JUST
BETWEEN
God
AND
ME

JUST
BETWEEN
God
AND
ME

Devotions for Young Adults

Sandra Drescher-Lehman

ZondervanPublishingHouse
Grand Rapids, Michigan

A Division of HarperCollinsPublishers

Just Between God and Me
Copyright © 1977, 1991 by Sandra Drescher-Lehman
All rights reserved
Requests for information should be addressed to:
Zondervan Publishing House
Grand Rapids, Michigan 49530

Library of Congress Cataloging-in-Publication Data

Drescher-Lehman, Sandra
　　[Just between God & me]
　　Just between God and me / Sandra Drescher-Lehman.
　　　　p.　cm.
　　Previously published under title: Just between God & me. 1977.
　　Summary: Includes a meditation, Scripture verse, and short prayer
for every day of the year.
　　ISBN 0-310-23881-1
　　1. Young adults—Prayer-books and devotions—English.
　　2. Devotional calendars. [1. Prayer books and devotions.]
　　I. Title.
　　BV4850.D74　1991
　　242'.63—dc20　　　　　　　　　　　　　　　　　　　　　91–3487
　　　　　　　　　　　　　　　　　　　　　　　　　　　　　　　CIP
　　　　　　　　　　　　　　　　　　　　　　　　　　　　　　　AC

All Scripture quotations, unless otherwise noted, are taken from the *Holy Bible: New International Version* (North American Edition). Copyright © 1973, 1978, 1984, by the International Bible Society. Used by permission of Zondervan Bible Publishers. Verses marked LB are from the *Living Bible*. Verses marked RSV are from the *Revised Standard Version*, and those marked NRSV are from the *New Revised Standard Version*.

Edited by Gerard Terpstra
Interior Design by Ann Cherryman
Cover design by Tammy Grabrian Johnson
Cover photo by Bill Binzen

Printed in the United States of America

98 99 00 01 02 /DC/ 18 17 16 15 14 13 12 11 10 9 8 7

To Dad,
who has given me love, guidance, and
encouragement in writing and growing,
and
to Mother,
who is one of my closest friends
in the adventure of discovering life.

Introduction

From as far back as I can remember, I have always wanted to write a book. I was at a loss, however, to know what I would write about. All the writers I knew were experts on their topics and were much older than I.

The summer after I graduated from high school, I was reading a devotional guide when the thought struck me that I could write a book like that. I was not an "expert Christian," but I could write about what I knew about God, and I had a relationship with Jesus that I could share. Since I loved to write, a devotional book seemed like a good way to share what I was experiencing.

For the next year, I took notes of what I thought and experienced in my relationship with God. I tried to look at my world through God's eyes. I tried to listen to the people and events around me for significant ideas to share. I tried to be aware of my own thoughts and feelings.

After my first year of college, I spent the summer elaborating on those notes, which eventually became my first book. I so enjoyed my "job" of being in touch with Jesus that I remember thinking it didn't really matter if anyone else ever saw what I had written.

Since that time, however, I have been grateful that others have read those devotionals. I have received letters from many people who said that a particular day's thought was just what they needed to hear from God. That assured me that I did not write it on my own. God knew what people would need to hear, and I felt honored to be used as God's messenger. I pray that with the new printing God's voice will continue to be heard above mine.

As a further guide to prayer, I have added a brief suggestion at the end of each devotional. They are intended to offer a concrete way to be in touch with God—sometimes in actions, sometimes in thought.

I have also added images that expand my earlier ideas of who God is. I am continually shown that God is far greater than my human imagination: all of life is a growing awareness of more aspects of God. I pray that each reader will use these words as a springboard to a unique and gratifying relationship with God.

CLEO FREELANCE PHOTO

A New Day　　　　　January 1

Father, I know that all my life
Is portioned out for me;
The changes that are sure to come
I do not fear to see;
I ask Thee for a present mind
Intent on pleasing Thee.

On this first day of the year these words by Henry Drummond have a special meaning for me. It's great to begin a year with the knowledge that the God who created me also travels with me and that I need not fear the future. Fear can creep in without an invitation and be paralyzing. But when I'm intent on pleasing God, there's less room for fear, and God strengthens me with faith for the day.

So do not fear, for I am with you; do not be dismayed, for I am your God. I will strengthen you and help you; I will uphold you with my righteous right hand. (Isa. 41:10)

Lord, since yesterday cannot be recalled and tomorrow cannot be assured, help me make the most of today. Teach me this coming year how to use each day for your glory and to know and do your will. Amen.

Commit the new year to God.

Starting Over　　　　　January 2

At the beginning of a new year the past is forgotten and new resolutions are made. It is easy to get carried away with all the festivities and make lots of grand promises about how I will live this year.

I know I need Jesus as I make these new beginnings. What I sometimes forget is that I need to go through every day with Jesus too. I need a greater strength than mine alone to carry out my intentions in the days ahead. When the days become monotonous and I feel insignificant, Jesus can bring new life and meaning.

And may your strength match the length of your days! (Deut. 33:25 LB)

Jesus, be with me throughout this new year as I learn to trust in you more and more. Teach me to receive the strength you give daily, so that each day can be more meaningful.

What do you resolve for the year ahead?

My Life—God's Story   January 3

My life is like a story, with God as its Author. I live my story with the same hours in a chapter as everyone else. Only the Author knows what will happen next; that makes it exciting!

Some chapters are sad and discouraging, but this makes the good chapters seem even better. Many conditions and characters are necessary to create a good story. Otherwise it would become unreal and boring.

The clue to getting the most enjoyment out of my story is to figure out what God is trying to communicate to me through each page and then to act on it. I've found that I'm happiest when I dwell on the good chapters rather than on the bitter, lonely ones; and I must remember to share the glory with God when others read part of my story and like it. After all, the character does not have a story to share without the Author!

You saw me before I was born and scheduled each day of my life before I began to breathe. Every day was recorded in your Book! (Ps. 139:16 LB)

God, you have made a good story for my life so far, and I trust you to continue writing it. Thank you for helping me create and live my role. Amen.

Give your "book" a title for the year ahead.

———◆◆————◆————◆◆———

Threads of Life   January 4

A poem I found describes in a slightly different way the feeling I expressed in yesterday's meditation.

Not until each loom is silent
And the shuttles cease to fly,
Will God unroll the pattern
And explain the reason why
The dark threads are so needful
In the Weaver's skillful hand
As the threads of gold and silver
For the pattern which He planned.

—Anonymous

Even though I don't understand why some moments in life are dark and miserable, God can find a use for them. With God's help I need to look for the beauty in them rather than just running away.

But when I am afraid, I will put my confidence in you. Yes, I will trust the promises of God. (Ps. 56:3–4 LB)

Thank you, Jesus, for taking care of my life so I don't need to worry. Help me to trust you more and more. Amen.

Notice the clouds today.

———◆◆————◆————◆◆———

Thy Will Be Done   January 5

My father keeps a short prayer in his date book. He told me he has carried it with him since his high school days when a friend first shared it with him.

> Renew my will from day to day,
> Blend it with Thine
> And take away
> All that now makes it hard to say
> Thy will be done.

Although the author is unknown, the prayer captures beautifully the deep desire of a committed Christian. It also has become the prayer I want to keep in my heart this new year.

Teach me to do your will, for you are my God. (Ps. 143:10)

Lord, help me to want the same things you know are good for my life. Each day may I sincerely say, "I delight in doing Your will." Amen.

How can your will for today be renewed?

Clowning for Christ   January 6

I met a woman yesterday who said she has a clown ministry. Dressed in her clown outfit and painted face, she spreads the joy she's found in Christ by making people laugh and feel good!

I had never thought before about being a clown with a specifically Christian message to tell, but it sounds like fun! It also makes me wonder about how many other ways God could use me if I'd open myself to the Creator to continue being creative through my life!

I always pray with joy because of your partnership in the gospel from the first day until now, being confident of this, that he who began a good work in you will carry it on to completion. (Phil. 1:4–6)

My wonderful Creator, fill me with your creative Spirit that always seeks new ways to share the joy of your love. Amen.

Imagine what you would look like as a clown.

———— •• —••— •• ————

Good Morning, Lord   January 7

Getting up each morning at the same time, going to school, rushing through classes and meals, doing homework, and going to bed—all that, only to get up the following day to the same routine, can get old! Is this the kind of life Christ wants for me?

Starting the day with a quiet time with the Lord makes a lot of difference in my life. The rest of my day can become a new adventure. Jesus' continual presence helps the events fall into place in a unique way. When I say, "Good morning, Lord! What do you have for us to do together today?" it makes every moment vibrant with expectancy and excitement. I am aware of who is directing each step.

In everything you do, put God first, and he will direct you and crown your efforts with success. (Prov. 3:6 LB)

Good morning, Lord! Thank you for being with me continually in everything I do. Let's go through this day together. Amen.

Talk to Jesus as you walk.

———— •• —••— •• ————

Real Worth

Many advertisements try to sell products that attempt to persuade me that I can become a better person by looking, feeling, or smelling a certain way. I get discouraged when I realize I've let myself be influenced by their propaganda. Advertisers seem to have missed the whole point of a person's worth. They insinuate that proper looks are more important than proper heart and actions, as Jesus teaches.

Jesus is far more interested in what kind of a person I am on the inside than merely what I appear to be on the outside.

All people are grass, their constancy is like the flower of the field. . . . The grass withers, the flower fades; but the word of our God will stand forever. (Isa. 40:6, 8 NRSV)

Lord, keep ever present in my mind the knowledge that outside beauty is only temporary. Inside beauty is what counts for eternity. Amen.

What do you have within that you hope never changes?

Walk Above the Waves

This morning I read the story in Matthew 14 of Peter's walk on the water. Peter was not aware of the waves as he began his journey toward Jesus. But when he thought about the potential danger, he became frightened and started to sink, crying out for the Lord's help. Immediately Jesus was there to rescue him.

That's how it is in my Christian life. When I keep my eyes fixed on Jesus, it's possible to live through difficulties and stay on top of my problems. I know that with Jesus by my side, they won't get the best of me. But as soon as I take my eyes off Jesus, and instead see only the dangerous winds and waves of life's trials, I begin to sink.

What's great is that each time I call for help, Jesus is right there, waiting patiently to lift me up again.

Immediately Jesus reached out his hand and caught him. "You of little faith," he said, "why did you doubt?" (Matt. 14:31)

Thank You, Jesus, for staying near to help me rise above the waves and not sink in every little storm. Amen.

What doubt do you have that Jesus can put to rest?

━━━━━━━●━●━━━━●━━━━━●━●━━━━━━━

Rich or Poor?   January 10

When I was small, I thought our family was poor. We didn't have a swimming pool or tennis courts as some of my friends did, and I wore lots of hand-me-down clothes.

Since then I've discovered that in a different and more important way, I am many times richer than those who are rich in material possessions alone. Whether or not I'm rich depends on how I view life and with whom I'm comparing myself.

I didn't bring anything into this world, and I can't take anything with me when I leave. No matter how long these years seem, time on earth is extremely short compared to eternity. This is home to me, but really I'm only a stranger living here for a while. My real and lasting home is in heaven. Therefore, true richness consists only of what is eternally important.

Riches are found in fellowship with good Christian friends and with God. I am rich when I have a loving family, the privilege of living where I'm free to worship God as I choose, a mind to think and reason, creativity to keep life exciting, and many other things. The world might not classify these as riches, but they are really the greatest riches anyone can attain.

What profit is there if you gain the whole world— and lose eternal life? What can be compared with the value of eternal life? (Matt. 16:26 LB)

Heavenly Keeper of my soul, help me to always strive for life's true riches and not get sidetracked into thinking the things of this world are most important. Help me to remember that only you can provide true riches. Amen.

Make a list of your "riches."

———••••———

God Still Speaks   January 11

The fact that God spoke to the prophets and other writers of the Bible more directly than to me today, sometimes becomes an excuse for me not to do something. I reason, "God didn't say it out loud from the sky, so how do I know for sure?"

Last year our class had an assignment to put ourselves in Abraham's place and write a first-person account of how he felt when God told him to sacrifice his only son, Isaac, as a burnt offering. One story suggested that maybe God just put the thought in Abraham's mind. Abraham had enough faith in God to do what he was told, even though it may not have come to him in an audible voice.

That made me wonder how concretely I'd have to hear God's voice to obey. I can know his will through the Bible, of course, and through the advice of Christian friends, as well as through God's convicting me. I hope I won't evade conviction just because God doesn't speak aloud to me.

I waited patiently for God to help me; then he listened and heard my cry. (Ps. 40:1 LB)

Let me know your wishes, God, in whatever way you think is best. Help me to know when and how you speak. Amen.

Listen for God's voice in others today.

———— •• ——•—— •• ————

Finding God's Will   January 12

Some time ago a friend and I were discussing how God speaks to us today. Neither of us had ever been spoken to by a voice from heaven. We knew God has ways of speaking directly to us, but sometimes it's hard to determine what is being said.

The next day we were traveling on an interstate highway. We didn't need gas right away, but we decided to stop anyway. After the service station attendant filled the gas tank, he noticed smoke coming from under the hood. He checked it, and the problem he found could have meant disaster if we had driven any farther. If we had stopped for gas earlier, however, it wouldn't have been noticeable yet.

We felt God had a hand in that situation and was showing us one of the ways he talks to us today. It was a good reminder to be aware of what God wants to tell me in whatever way he might choose.

Many blessings are given to those who trust the Lord. (Ps. 40:4 LB)

Thank you, Lord, for speaking to me today. Help me to know when it's you talking, or if my selfish desires are getting mixed up with your desires. Amen.

Listen for God's voice through the ordinary events of your day.

———— •• ——•—— •• ————

I'm Responsible for Me   January 13

When I'm trying to decide what to do, a big consideration for me is what my friends are doing. That's not always bad, but I'm beginning to see that it can be. It's easy to disregard my own values and think something can't be wrong if so many of my friends are doing it.

While friends, especially Christian friends, can be of help, it is most important to remember that when God looks at my life, how many others have done the same things is not taken into account. I alone am responsible for my actions, words, and thoughts. I must keep what I do in perspective with what God wants of me, without blindly following others.

So then, each of us will give an account of himself to God. (Rom. 14:12)

I am looking to you, my loving Judge, for guidance in my daily walk with you. Amen.

Think about a decision you need to make. What advice would your friends give? What advice does your Best Friend give?

Magnify the Lord   January 14

Binoculars are fun to use. With them, distant objects become much larger and clearer, as though I am closer to them. When the Bible talks of magnifying the name of the Lord, I can compare it with how things are magnified through binoculars.

Christ's ways can't really be enlarged or made stronger, but I can bring them closer in my mind. When I cut out the background, foreground, and sideviews—which distract me from focusing my attention on Christ alone—I can see divine ways more clearly, as though we are drawn closer together.

Jesus remains the same, waiting for me to adjust my binoculars.

Christ shall be magnified in my body, whether it be by life, or by death. (Phil. 1:20 KJV)

Jesus, I want to learn better how to magnify you. Teach me to focus on you alone. Amen.

Look closely at a tree—and magnify the Creator.

A Help in Trouble January 15

A woman came to church with an exciting story to tell. She had been watching an ant carry a piece of straw. The straw was small, but it was large compared to the ant. The ant came to a channel of water, also tiny, but dangerous for the ant. Instead of giving up or turning back, the ant put the straw down, crawled across the water on it, picked up the straw, and went on!

The story reminded me of how my life must look in God's eyes. I face many situations that look dangerous and threatening to me, but God sees how easily I could overcome the problem and gives me wisdom and strength. God doesn't allow me to face any situation that is impossible for me to handle but helps me find a way over the deep spots.

Take a lesson from the ants, you lazy fellow. Learn from their ways and be wise! (Prov. 6:6 LB)

Thank you, Lord, for caring so much about me and helping me through all of life's trials. Amen.

Pay attention to the small things in life today.

Letting God Use Me   January 16

A few years ago, a building near us was condemned because termites had eaten so much wood that the building wasn't safe any more. Later it was torn down because nothing could be done with it. The termites had completely destroyed it.

It's amazing to think that something as small as a termite can do so much damage! When I think about the vastness of our world and universe, I feel small and insignificant; but the termites taught me a good lesson. Everything I do has some impact, and it's up to me to determine whether it's good or bad. If little termites can ruin a big building, I can do something far greater for good if I'm willing to work at it.

God can use the smallest deeds of goodness. Even if no one else sees it, God will reward fully.

May the LORD repay you for what you have done. May you be richly rewarded by the LORD, the God of Israel, under whose wings you have come to take refuge. (Ruth 2:12)

Dear God, help me to think about what good I can do, instead of feeling small and insignificant. Amen.

Imagine comforting yourself under God's wings.

What a Friend!   January 17

The blind poet George Matheson wrote:

> *There is an Eye that never sleeps*
> *Beneath the wing of night;*
> *There is an Ear that never shuts*
> *When sink the beams of light;*
> *There is an Arm that never tires*

When human strength gives way;
There is a Love that never fails
When earthly loves decay.

It's almost too unbelievable to know that I have such a friend!

How precious it is, Lord, to realize that you are thinking about me constantly! I can't even count how many times a day your thoughts turn towards me. (Ps. 139:17 LB)

God, your constant love overwhelms me! How can I begin to praise you enough? Amen.

Close your eyes and imagine being totally relaxed in Jesus' arms.

Fruit of the Spirit　　　January 18

Recently I made a surprising discovery. In reading about the fruit of the Holy Spirit, I noticed that *fruit* is always written in the singular. That indicates that each Christian has been given some of each fruit and not just a little of one or two.

Unlike the gifts of the Spirit—one Christian usually doesn't have all of the gifts—I am responsible, by the Holy Spirit's power, to nurture each fruit and allow it to grow. Bearing fruit is a quiet, steady process, flourishing best in situations where I relate to others who are also growing Spirit fruit. By producing the fruit of the Spirit in greater abundance, the Holy Spirit's presence in my life becomes more evident.

But when the Holy Spirit controls our lives he will produce this kind of fruit in us: love, joy, peace, patience, kindness, goodness, faithfulness, gentleness and self-control; and here there is no conflict with Jewish laws (Gal. 5:22 LB).

Dear God, I pray that your Spirit will work freely in my life to strengthen the fruit of love, joy, peace, patience, kindness, goodness, faithfulness, gentleness, and self-control. Amen.

Pull out a weed that is choking the growth of your Spirit fruit.

More Fruit   January 19

Like the trees and vines that produce fruit, when I'm growing Spirit fruit, I need to be pruned in order to produce to my best potential. When I sincerely ask for more of any one fruit, I can expect trying situations to help that fruit to mature. I recall a time when I prayed for patience to become more real in me. In the weeks that followed, God put many situations in my life that tested my patience. They weren't easy, but I know they came as God's loving response to my prayer.

Pruning can be painful, but it is necessary for the best and fullest production. Christ prunes me as I need it and as I'm ready.

Since we live by the Spirit, let us keep in step with the Spirit. (Gal. 5:25)

Thank you, Lord, for helping me grow the fruit of your Spirit. Don't spare me the pain of pruning, but teach me your ways. Amen.

Let the food you eat today remind you of the fruit growing in your life.

Pruning   January 20

Every year after our grapes, cherries, and roses are done bearing, my dad prunes them. He cuts them down so far it's hard to believe they will ever grow again, but it actually helps them produce more.

God does the same thing in my life. When one task or opportunity in my life is accomplished, it is often taken away in order to make room for the next one. Sometimes I long to be the same person I was yesterday. But God knows when it's time for me to move on—to produce strength in new areas as well.

I have to remember that God cuts away out of love—to help me have more strength and usefulness in other places. Pruning away useless branches is a necessary part of growth if I want to produce more and better fruit. And being the perfect Gardener, God never prunes me more than I can handle.

He cuts off every branch in me that bears no fruit, while every branch that does bear fruit he prunes so that it will be even more fruitful. (John 15:2)

Savior, prune away the fruitless part of me as much as you think is right, and give me the strength to produce more fruit for you. Amen.

Think about the different things in which you've been fruitful over the past several years. Celebrate them!

A Simple Lifestyle   January 21

José Ortiz is a brilliant young Puerto Rican Christian leader who has come to the United States to lead the Spanish churches. Recently at a conference I heard him speak about the Christian lifestyle of simple living. He described the Christian lifestyle as simply "caring more about persons than things."

A person may live in a hut with few of life's possessions yet be a miser and unconcerned about others. Poverty, or the denial of things, in itself, is hardly Christian.

Putting people ahead of things determines how I use my time, my money, and my possessions, and this results in a certain lifestyle. As a Christian called to a simple lifestyle, I might consider what I can do for others instead of dreading giving up what I ought to.

Blessed are the poor in spirit, for theirs is the kingdom of heaven. (Matt. 5:3)

Lord, grant that I may seek to serve people and not care so much about things. Instill in me a true sense of caring for others. Amen.

Memorize Matthew 5:3.

Why Worry?   January 22

In all the activity of school, home, and church life, I tend to worry a lot about how I'll get things done and whether or not everything will work out right. It may seem to an observer that I translate the verse that says, "Don't worry about tomorrow for your heavenly Father will take care of you" into "Worry all day about tomorrow, for if you don't, nothing will work out."

Too often I forget that God has promised to take care of all my problems. It's actually an insult to God for me to worry, because I'm saying, "God, I don't think you can handle this situation, so I'm going to worry about it."

Let him have all your worries and cares, for he is always thinking about you and watching everything that concerns you. (1 Peter 5:7 LB)

Thank you, Lord, for being my constant protector. You know what is best for me. Keep me trusting in you instead of worrying. Amen.

Write down one of your worries and throw away the paper as a symbol of giving up that worry.

Wasted Worry   January 23

Not only is worry needless for a Christian, but it's also a waste of time. Someone wrote of worry:

40% will never happen, for anxiety is the result of a tired mind;

30% concerns old decisions that cannot be altered;

12% centers on criticisms, mostly untrue, made by people who feel inferior;

10% is related to my health, which worsens while I worry, and only

8% is "legitimate," showing that life does have real problems, which may be met head on when I have eliminated senseless worries.

Many of us spend half our time wishing for things we could have if we didn't spend half our time wishing. As Philipp Melanchthon once said, "Trouble and perplexity drive us to prayer, and prayer drives away trouble and perplexity."

Don't worry about anything; instead, pray about everything; tell God your needs and don't forget to thank him for his answers. (Phil. 4:6 LB)

With you, O God, I can see what a waste of time it is for me to worry. Help me to stay away from the sin of worry. Amen.

Write down another worry you have, give it to God, and watch how God uses it.

Turn Worry into Faith   January 24

Worry can have a positive perspective. It can prove that I really am interested in a friend or person God has brought into my life or that I really care about a situation. Knowing what to do with my concern or worry for that person is what's important.

If I turn my worry into faith, my faith can be as strong as my worry was. One prayer does more good than many times that amount of time spent worrying. I need to pray for the faith necessary to control or overcome worry. To make the most of my worry, I can turn its energy into faith in God to work everything out.

His peace will keep your thoughts and your hearts quiet and at rest as you trust in Christ Jesus. (Phil. 4:7 LB)

Give me the ability, Jesus, to turn all my useless worry into a strong, powerful faith so that I may be closer to you. Amen.

Write down a third worry and an idea about how God could use it to strengthen your faith. Put it in your Bible.

What Is Faith?   January 25

Leslie D. Weatherhead, in his book *The Transforming Friendship*, tells an interesting story.

An old Scotsman found it impossible to pray. When he tried, his thoughts wandered or he fell asleep. He became so worried that he spoke to his minister about it. The minister advised him to put a chair beside him, imagine Jesus sitting in the chair, and talk as he would to a friend. By doing this, the Scotsman accepted the gift of companionship and made his Friend real, not by intellect or will, but by an imagination that became faith. When he died, his arm was resting on the empty chair beside him.

Faith is believing Jesus is with me all the time and accepting his friendship as a gift. As the spelling of *faith* may suggest: Forsaking All, I Take Him. I have faith when I am willing to give my friendship with Jesus top priority in my life.

The righteous will live by faith. (Rom. 1:17)

Gentle Friend, guide me in your ways. Be real to me so my faith will grow in you. Thank you. Amen.

Pray with your hands open to receive Jesus.

The Gift of Salvation   January 26

Giving gifts is fun. I love to see the joy of a child when he or she is given a gift and the joy of the giver for being able to cheer up another person's day.

I've also seen the hurt that comes when a gift is rejected. When someone is not willing to accept even the smallest gift of kindness, joy is taken out of the giving. Jesus has a greater gift to give each of us than we can comprehend—the gift of salvation. We don't need to earn it or prove our worthiness. Joy comes in simple acceptance and gratitude.

Thanks be to God for his indescribable gift! (2 Cor. 9:15)

Thank you, Savior, for giving me the gift of salvation.
Amen.

Spend a minute reflecting on what this gift means to you.

Walking with Jesus   January 27

When I was a child, each day before I ran to the bus stop for school, I prayed this short prayer with my mother:

Starting out this morning, this is what I pray,
Take my hand, dear Jesus, walk with me today.
Then I'll just go places where you wish me to.
I'll be safe and happy, hand in hand with you.

The prayer remained with me as I grew older, but it has added meaning. Now I have a clearer understanding of what it means to walk each day, hand in hand with Jesus. It feels good to have someone to keep me safe and happy— someone who will never leave me. It feels good to have the knowledge of Jesus' constant guidance.

I am the LORD, your God, who takes hold of your right hand and says to you, Do not fear; I will help you. (Isa. 41:13)

Take my hand, dear Jesus, and walk with me today. I'll be safe and happy, hand in hand with you. Amen.

Write a short prayer of your own, committing this day to God.

Living Moment by Moment

When the fourth person from my high school class was suddenly killed in a car accident, I along with others began to take a new look at life. Death was no longer something that happened to someone else in the distant future.

I began to examine my priorities in life and question whether or not they were really important. Questions like these became very real: If I had one day left on earth, would I be living the same way and doing the same things as I am now? Could any relationships be improved? Do my friends and family know how much I appreciate them? And most important—is my relationship with God what I want it to be?

Our lives are so unpredictable. We can't look ahead and think we'll take care of something tomorrow or next week. Living one moment at a time and doing what is eternally significant right now is most important.

Lord, help me to realize how brief my time on earth will be. Help me to know that I am here for but a moment more. (Ps. 39:4 LB)

God, I love you. I want to live for you, and that means doing what you want me to do every moment of my life. Guide me in making the right decisions. Amen.

Think about today as if it were your last one here on earth.

My Face—A Mirror

It's fun to watch people. By looking at their faces, I can usually tell how they're feeling inside. Faces are like mirrors, reflecting what's going on underneath.

It's easy to forget how much my face tells about me and think no one else will notice. It's not too hard to look happy when I *am* happy; but when I'm *not* happy—that's when the real test comes. Sometimes it's hard to smile, but it's not fair to make others miserable just because I'm feeling a little down. As Myron Augsburger once said, "A forced smile is better than a sincere grouch."

And we, who with unveiled faces all reflect the Lord's glory, are being transformed into his likeness with ever-increasing glory, which comes from the Lord, who is the Spirit. (2 Cor. 3:18)

Joy-Giver, may I learn to let your joy radiate from my face, even when I'm not feeling it myself. Amen.

Smile at yourself in the mirror.

━━━━━◆━━◆━━◆━━━━━

Peace   *January 30*

Saint Francis of Assisi penned a powerful prayer on peace—a prayer that is a great challenge to me:

Lord,
    make me an instrument of your peace.
    Where there is hatred let me sow love;
    Where there is injury, pardon;
    Where there is despair, hope;
    Where there is darkness, light; and
    Where there is sadness, joy.

O divine Master,
    grant that I may not so much
    Seek to be consoled as to console;
    To be understood as to understand;
    To be loved as to love;
    For it is in giving that we receive;

It is in pardoning that we are pardoned; and
It is in dying that we are born to eternal life.

The rising sun will come . . . to shine on those living
in darkness and in the shadow of death, to guide
our feet into the path of peace. (Luke 1:78–79)

Lord, may the prayer of Saint Francis be mine. Amen.

Choose one phrase from the above prayer to repeat
throughout the day.

Memory—
Good or Bad?   January 31

A good memory is useful when cramming for a test,
learning lines for a play, memorizing Scripture, or listening to
a lecture without needing to take notes.

However, a good memory can be a problem if too many
of the wrong things are remembered. That single cutting
remark made in one short moment may be remembered for
months. A careless comment made by a best friend can ruin a
relationship if it's dwelt on rather than quickly forgiven and
forgotten. Too many memories of someone you've dated in
the past can result in a fantasy world if you don't face the
reality that it's over. Memories will live on, but you can't live
on memories.

Memories are good if they don't become a way of life.
Right now life is too exciting to keep looking back.

I am bringing all my energies to bear on this one
thing: Forgetting the past and looking forward to
what lies ahead. (Phil. 3:13 LB)

Enable me, O Lord, to blot from my memory past
remarks or events that serve only to nourish bitterness. Help

me to press onward each day anew, and not be continually reminded of the past. Amen.

In a moment of quiet meditation, thank God for the gifts of this day.

———————————

Stay Nourished   February 1

Our garden was growing well last summer. Everything was green, and the vegetables were developing beautifully. Then we had a drought, and the plants began to wilt. Their roots hadn't grown deep enough to remain healthy. They didn't receive the nourishment they needed to survive.

As I think about my life, I find it much like a garden. As long as I have the proper nourishment from Christ, I continue to grow, developing deeper, stronger roots in a life of following Christ. If that source is cut off, however, I quickly lose health and strength in my Christian life. The best way to be assured of continual growth is to spend time each day getting spiritual nourishment by reading about who Jesus was and by talking with Jesus about who I can be, as I continue to grow in him.

Let your roots grow down into him and draw up nourishment from him. See that you go on growing in the Lord, and become strong and vigorous in the truth you were taught. (Col. 2:7 LB)

Thank you, O Christ, for providing the nourishment I need to become strong spiritually. Help me to grow deep roots in living continually with you. Amen.

Review your New Year's resolutions.

Branches and Vines   February 2

As I think further about spiritual nourishment, the analogy of Jesus as the Vine and myself as a branch comes to my mind. A branch cannot live and grow unless it is attached to and is receiving nourishment from the vine. Only in keeping that contact can the branch hope to bear fruit.

My life works the same way. I can't survive on my own strength. I need Jesus Christ, as the Vine, to be attached to and to help me grow. After being supplied by Jesus for all my needs, I can produce a large crop of fruit, something that would be impossible if I tried to do it on my own.

If I would be separate from Jesus, my spiritual life would wither and be useless.

I am the vine, you are the branches. Those who abide in me and I in them bear much fruit, because apart from me you can do nothing. Whoever does not abide in me is thrown away like a branch and withers; such branches are gathered, thrown into the fire, and burned. (John 15:5–6 NRSV)

You are the Vine, Jesus, and I want to be your branch, depending on you for everything. Keep me attached to you so I won't wither and die. Amen.

Gaze at a piece of fruit and reflect on the process of its growth.

Life Sculpture   *February 3*

Michelangelo was asked how he did such a good job on his sculpture of David, to make it look so real. He replied that he had just chiseled away everything that wasn't David.

Jesus can be that kind of sculptor in my life. As I allow it, Christ will chisel away all that isn't Christlike. Some of the chiseling and polishing may be hard to take or hard for me to see the need for, but they're necessary in order to have the sculpture of my life look as much like Jesus as possible.

Do not conform any longer to the pattern of this world, but be transformed by the renewing of your mind. (Rom. 12:2)

I pray, Lord, that I will keep turning my life over to you, so you can turn this sculpture into something that everyone will know is patterned after you. Amen.

Write a list of your plans for the day. Chisel away all that is not Christlike.

My Constant Friend   February 4

When I was younger, my best friend lived just down the road from us. We talked, played, and went everywhere together. Then she moved away. We wrote and visited each other, but it wasn't often enough to keep our friendship close. When we got together after that, we knew that our relationship wasn't the same as before.

My relationship with God works the same way. When we spend time talking together, I become more sensitive to who God is, and our relationship is close. If I slack off, our relationship slacks off too. But I am thankful that God always waits for me and welcomes me back.

My God is changeless in his love for me and he will come and help me. (Ps. 59:10 LB)

Thank you, Lord, that you are a constant friend, even when I'm unfaithful. I pray that I will always remain aware of your love and care. Amen.

What do you expect of a friend?

Start Exploring   February 5

While reading part of an article written by Atlee Beachy, a college professor and counselor, I was struck by the following words: "Your young years are years to explore, a time to discuss doubts and to examine your beliefs. Your temptation may be, however, to delay, to put off making a basic commitment. You may rationalize your delay by saying you are searching. You may delay moving into life until suddenly you discover that life is passing you by. You may throw off traditions and beliefs before affirming a new faith."

It's not always easy for me to think about what I believe and make decisions about what I value. Sometimes I'd rather just be a child a while longer and not think seriously about life. But that kind of an attitude can set a life pattern of not ever seriously considering the important decisions. To make life more meaningful now and for the future, the present is the best time to think about my beliefs, doubts, fears, and values, and to explore what really has meaning for my life.

Don't let the excitement of being young cause you to forget about your Creator. (Eccl. 12:1 LB)

Lord, I'm ready to take you seriously and to let you be a real part of my life now and as I grow up. Live in me and help me make the necessary decisions. Amen.

What can you commit to God today?

———••————•————••———

Being a Faithful Servant   February 6

Sometimes the jobs assigned to me are so small and insignificant that they hardly seem worth doing. But as I do the minor jobs faithfully, I find that the responsibilities given to me become broader and more challenging. And I can see that the first experiences were necessary in order to do a good job at bigger tasks.

Children learn to run after they've first learned to walk. God works the same way in my life. The grandeur and importance of my job is not as significant as how well I carry out whatever responsibility I have been given.

For everyone who has will be given more, and he will have an abundance. Whoever does not have, even what he has will be taken from him. (Matt. 25:29)

May I always do the best with what I have, Jesus, to prepare me for even greater responsibilities. Amen.

Commit the smallest task of the day to God.

Help Me, Lord   February 7

Help me, Lord! I can't win this race alone. I'm too tired. Help me to remember all I learned and pass my exam today. Help me to learn all my lines for this play. Help me keep my patience through all this confusion.

These kinds of "help me" prayers have filled my days. I thought God was glad to be included in my problems. But then another thought struck me. Where was God when I passed the exams, when I did win the race? I've tended to forget God when I was joyful and to send out emergency prayers when I needed help.

God wants to meet my needs, but we both also enjoy prayers of praise and thanksgiving.

Think about all you can praise God for and be glad about. (Phil. 4:8 LB)

Glorious Giver, thank you for being near and waiting patiently for me to grow up. Thank you for the many good things you have given me. Amen.

Count your blessings.

Be an Individual February 8

A girl once wrote to a glamour columnist saying that she felt inferior to the girls around her because she dressed differently. The columnist's advice to the girl was that she be herself and not try to copy everyone else—because each person has her own individuality.

God has given each person something special that no one else has. This special individuality should not be suppressed but put to work for everyone's advantage. Only by developing my own unique personality will I ever be able to feel good about myself. God intended me to be an original, not a carbon copy of someone else.

And steadfast love belongs to you, O Lord. For you repay to all according to their work. (Ps. 62:12 NRSV)

Lord, thank you for making me different from everyone else. Grant that I will always put my individuality to its best use for your work. Amen.

Think of one way you are unique.

For the Glory of God February 9

Brother Lawrence was a 16th-century monk who practiced doing everything in his life for the glory of God. He was reportedly assigned to work in the kitchen. It was an assignment he didn't enjoy, but in spite of that he decided that he would flip each egg cake for the glory of God. He even picked up each straw from the floor for the glory of God.

Life can take on new meaning and importance when each thing is done and each moment is lived for the glory of God!

Rejoice in the Lord always. I will say it again: Rejoice! (Phil. 4:4)

Thank you, my God, for the reminder of your glory.

Think of a repetitious task or event in your day. Let it be a reminder to you of living every moment for the glory of God!

--------•--◆--•--------

Right or Wrong?   February 10

In high school I started to make many of my own decisions. Mother and Dad weren't always near to see what choices I made and to tell me whether something was the right thing to do. I enjoyed the freedom, but along with freedom came responsibility.

It can be difficult for a Christian to decide what is right and what is wrong. Four guidelines a friend had written in the back of her Bible have helped me:
1. Don't go anywhere you wouldn't want to go with Jesus.
2. Don't do anything you wouldn't want to do with Jesus.
3. Don't say anything you wouldn't want to say to Jesus.
4. Don't think anything you wouldn't want to think with Jesus.

Whoever says, "I abide in him," ought to walk just as he walked. (1 John 2:6 NRSV)

Keep instilled within me, Lord, the ability to know right from wrong. Guide me in everything I do, say, or think, that all will be for your glory. Amen.

Go through your day aware of Jesus at your side.

--------•--◆--•--------

Why Do You Serve?   February 11

I recently read a short article entitled, "Why Do You Serve?" The author wrote, "If we serve God because we fear

God, we are slaves. If we serve God because we feel we ought to, then we are servants. But if we serve God because we love God, we become sons and daughters."

God doesn't want to be a slavemaster, but a loving Father. Like a good parent, God wants our actions to blossom out of our love, rather than guilt or obligation. Then we are freed to serve!

Say "Thank you" to the Lord for being so good, for always being so loving and kind. (Ps. 107:1 LB)

Thank you for creating me to be one of your children. You are so good. Amen.

Pay attention to your image of God.

———◆——◆——◆———

Finding the Fault of Faultfinding
February 12

The title of this meditation was also the title of an editorial in our school newspaper. It caught my attention. Its premise, with which I could readily identify, is that it's easier to find the faults of people, school, church, and community rather than to seek out their good qualities.

But I'm convinced that Christ's way is to look for the good. We don't need to be so naïve that we don't recognize evil, but more than enough people grumble about bad conditions. Jesus was sent into the world to bring peace and love abundantly. We are now Christ's messengers on earth and therefore have a responsibility to let love and goodness shine through us to others.

An optimist is more fun to be around than a faultfinder.

To the pure, all things are pure, but to those who are corrupted and do not believe, nothing is pure. (Titus 1:15)

I want to be like you, Jesus. I want to spread your love and peace, instead of complaining and finding fault. With your help I know I can do it. Amen.

Give a sincere compliment.

------◆◆◆◆◆------

Let Go   *February 13*

A farmer saw a cat fall into a well, and he hurried over to rescue it. When he looked down into the well, he saw that the cat was clinging to a ledge to prevent a further drop. The farmer quickly lowered a bucket into the well, but the cat wouldn't fall into it. Finally, when the cat could hold on no longer, it let go and fell into the bucket, and the farmer rescued it.

Sometimes I am like the cat. When I get myself into scary situations, God just waits for me to fall into the safe and loving arms that await me. Trusting God completely can be scary, but not as scary as the only alternative—doing it alone!

My eyes are fixed on you, O Sovereign LORD; in you I take refuge. (Ps. 141:8)

Thank you, Savior, for being always near to rescue me from the situations I run into. I'm sorry for the times when I don't let go completely and trust you. Amen.

Let God carry you today.

------◆◆◆◆◆------

The Joy of Giving   *February 14*

Two days before Valentine's Day our school exchanged names, and in this way our "Secret Hearts" were determined. Each person was given an opportunity to do something special for the person whose name he or she had picked. On Valentine's Day shouts of joy and happy faces lined the halls and filled the classrooms as students found such things as anonymous valentines, cookies, candy, decorated lockers, balloons, and cakes. The mood of the entire school was brightened because of these simple acts of kindness.

That day reminded `me of the joy that comes from showing people I care. Valentine's Day is a great time for showing friends how much I love them, but then so are the other 364 days in the year!

In response to all he has done for us, let us outdo each other in being helpful and kind to each other and in doing good. (Heb. 10:24 LB)

Thank you, greatest Love, for being so kind and for giving me the gift of kindness. Grant that I will never stifle the urge to do a favor or pass up a chance to make someone happier. Amen.

Make heart-shaped cookies for your friends.

———— •◗ ◖•◗ •◗ ————

Give Freely   February 15

At home Mother has a bulletin board where she posts articles and thoughts that may be helpful or interesting. One week I discovered one that was both thought-provoking and challenging.

The happy ones are those who:

Give love rather than expect love.

Reach out to others rather than expecting to be reached out to.

Desire to be a friend more than to have friends.

Express appreciation rather than expect appreciation.

Love to relieve suffering rather than think of their own suffering.

Think on others' good points rather than ponder failings.

Pray "God bless others" more than "God bless me."

Give freely without thought of being given to.

Are more conscious of their neglect of others than of others' neglect of them.

Have forgotten themselves in doing things which are remembered.

Each of you must give as you have made up your mind, not reluctantly or under compulsion, for God loves a cheerful giver. (2 Cor. 9:7 NRSV)

Thank you for giving me so much, Lord. I pray that I may always be ready to give with a willing heart. Amen.

From the above list pick out one phrase to consciously practice today.

One Step at a Time   February 16

When my brother came home from his first day in kindergarten, he announced that he wasn't going back because he hadn't learned how to read or how to play the piano. He was too young to realize that those things take time to learn.

The same thing can happen in our Christian lives. We have so much to learn about God that it will take our whole lives to soak it in. Yet sometimes everything looks too complicated, and giving up seems like the easiest way out.

God doesn't expect me to learn everything at once any more than a child can learn everything on the first day of school. I must simply trust God to continue to lead me one step at a time.

Do your best to present yourself to God as one approved by him, a worker who has no need to be ashamed, rightly explaining the word of truth. (2 Tim. 2:15 NRSV)

Give me patience, Lord, to follow your leading and not look ahead to where others may be. Amen.

What is the step you will take today in learning to know God better?

———•——•——•———

A Christian— a Witness   February 17

Is it possible for others to know I'm a Christian by their being in school with me for a week? A month? A year?

When I was asked that question, it made me think. In what ways do I let others know whom I serve? I never went witnessing door to door or passed out tracts or led a Bible study.

Then I thought about some of my Christian friends and how they witness. I discovered they did it in many ways—for example, by being available when a friend or neighbor is in need, or by kindness and patience when talking with people. Some Christians are preachers and teachers, while others live their faith more quietly. I am always a witness to those I come in contact with each day. To be a nonwitnessing Christian is impossible. I'm not a lesser Christian because my way of witnessing isn't the same as my brothers' and sisters'.

And how can we be sure that we belong to him? By looking within ourselves: are we really trying to do what he wants us to? (I John 2:3 LB)

Use me, Lord, as your witness in whatever way you need me. Keep me ever mindful of your presence within me so I may portray you to others. Amen.

Look at your life as an outsider might see it. How is Christ evident?

----••----■----■----•----

God Is Always Near   February 18

When I was small, I was afraid of the dark. Mother always told me that God was right beside me and there was no need to be afraid, but I was afraid anyway.

Recently, as a friend talked with me about Psalm 139, I began to realize in a new way how close God is to me all the time. No darkness is too dark, no place too far away, no thought too secret, no action too small, to hide from God.

I find a lot of comfort in the fact that such a great and wonderful God is always there for me. I can't think or do anything without God's knowing! That's ultimate caring!

This is too glorious, too wonderful to believe! I can never be lost to your Spirit! I can never get away from my God! (Ps. 139:6–7 LB)

Wonderful Savior, help me to be more aware of and more thankful for your continual presence. Amen.

Write a love note to God.

----••----■----■----•----

Honorable Parents   February 19

"Honor your father and mother." Any time I'm tempted to disregard that command, I can remind myself of these things:

• My parents, along with God, were partners in my creation.

- They spent countless hours day and night, comforting me as a crying infant, cooking for me, washing me, and just spending time with me.
- Large amounts of their money have gone to my care.
- They have allowed me to make many mistakes; so I should allow them to make a few too. After all, they're only human, like me.
- God commanded me to honor and obey them.

The last reminder makes sense. Anyone who has done as much for me as my parents have deserves my love, respect, and praise. It may seem difficult at times, but they've loved me when it was difficult too!

"Honor your father and mother"—which is the first commandment with a promise—"that it may go well with you and that you may enjoy long life on the earth." (Eph. 6:2–3)

O God, thank you for my parents. Let me always be aware of them as people who love me so much that they're giving a big part of their lives for me. Amen.

Tell your parents what you appreciate about them.

———— ••▬••• ————

Serve Today   February 20

I was listening to a presentation by the Christian Young Peoples Association. They were asking for volunteers to help with mentally disabled persons, jail visitation, young children, and people in nursing homes. The ideas all sounded good, but I decided to wait until next year, because this year I would be too busy.

Then the speaker's words cut into my thoughts. He said that if our excuse is that we're too busy, that's the way it's going to be for the rest of our lives. We must begin serving the Lord today, and that means making time in our schedules. God's work can't be put off!

Teach us to number our days and recognize how few they are; help us to spend them as we should. (Ps. 90:12 LB)

Teach me, Lord, the wisest use of my time. May I never be too busy to serve you. Amen.

Do your day's plans include service to others?

———————————

Loneliness   February 21

Loneliness is an emotion that can spoil the good things in life for days, weeks, and even months if I let it.

I was lonely at a retreat with thirty other kids my age.

I was lonely in the midst of a family who cared about me. I was lonely at school with people all around.

My dad and I were talking about the causes of loneliness. He said that often loneliness stems from self-centeredness. I began to analyze some of the times I had been lonely and found, to my surprise, that he was right.

My loneliness couldn't be blamed on anyone else, because each time I was done feeling sorry for myself and decided to get back into the mainstream of life, my friends were still there waiting to accept me back. I must be willing to stop feeling sorry for myself long enough to see past my own selfishness.

Lord, when doubts fill my mind, when my heart is in turmoil, quiet me and give me renewed hope and cheer. (Ps. 94:19 LB)

Lord, thank you for showing me the causes of loneliness. With your help, I want to reach out to others rather than think only of myself. Amen.

Visit a lonely neighbor.

Overcoming Loneliness   February 22

After I discovered what causes loneliness, I began to think of ways to overcome it. By admitting loneliness, I was really saying, "I can't think of anyone but myself."

Therefore, to overcome loneliness one must think of others. Ideas came to my mind such as baking something for a sick neighbor, sending a note of appreciation to a teacher, or just spending time talking to someone. After a few experiences of reaching out, I realized the truth of this cure. The joy of giving of myself to others took the lonely feelings away.

Do to others what you would have them do to you. (Matt. 7:12)

Lord, when I'm feeling lonely, help me to recognize my selfish attitude and get rid of it by doing something for someone else. Amen.

Put yourself in another's shoes.

Plant God's Word Deep   February 23

The parable of the sower was always an interesting story to me, but recently a friend gave me a new insight that made it more meaningful: Like the seed in the parable, I need to let God's message sink deep into my heart and produce fruit in the way I live and love others.

If, like the birds in the parable, worry and doubt enter my life and try to take away God's message, I can do something about it. Rather than spending my time chasing the birds away, I should plant God's Word deep enough in my heart that I can doubt without letting my doubt shake the roots of my faith.

In this world other forces will always be present. Only when I have God's Word planted deep within can I withstand the pressure.

But as for what was sown on good soil, this is the one who hears the word and understands it, who indeed bears fruit and yields, in one case a hundredfold, in another sixty, and in another thirty (Matt. 13:23 NRSV)

God, I pray that your Word will be planted so deep within me that nothing can take it away. Produce fruit in my relationships as I continue to live and love. Amen.

Write down one thing about God that you're sure of.

————— ••———•——— • —————

Don't Complain, Give Thanks   *February 24*

A friend once told me, "If, for one day, I was in your shoes, I'd be happy." That surprised me. I hadn't realized my circumstances were that good.

After thinking about it, I realized how much I have to be thankful for that I had been taking for granted. I can't remember thanking God for my internal organs, although if I didn't have them I'd be in poor shape. It's easier to complain than to be thankful. We say, "My nose is too long" instead of "I'm glad I can smell," "I wish I had longer legs" instead of "I'm glad I can walk."

Who am I to tell my Creator that I don't like how I was made? God didn't make a mistake. This world would be boring if everyone looked alike and had the same talents. The sooner I stop complaining, the more time I'll have to be thankful and build on the gifts I've been given.

Always give thanks for everything to our God and Father in the name of our Lord Jesus Christ. (Eph. 5:20 LB)

My gracious Lord, thank you for making me just as I am. Guard me from any desire to change what I cannot change, and help me to accept myself as you made me. Amen.

Acknowledge two things you like about yourself.

———◆◆—◆——◆◆———

Believe and Obey   February 25

As I was reading Dietrich Bonhoeffer's book *The Cost of Discipleship*, I came across this proposition: "Only those who believe obey and only those who obey believe." Bonhoeffer went on to say that belief without obedience or obedience without belief doesn't save a person. Both are necessary.

Sometimes it's easy for me to focus all my attention on doing the right things as if doing them will save me. Other times I get lazy in thinking I'm saved by God's grace when I believe, without having to do anything in response. But it's only when his grace and my obedience are working together that I can be used for God's purposes.

As the body without the spirit is dead, so faith without deeds is dead. (James 2:26)

Savior, keep me from concentrating too much on obedience to believe and from thinking that belief without obedience is enough. Amen.

What is your response to God's great love?

———◆◆—◆——◆◆———

Stubborn Doubts   February 26

When I have something planned and I can see clearly how everything is going to work out, it's easy to become impatient with those who hesitate to give their cooperation because they don't understand everything completely.

That makes me wonder how God has so much patience with me. There are lots of times when I hesitate, thinking I need to know more of the details first. And God waits until I'm willing to go on. God sees the way clearly and yet does not pull me through like a puppet. God does, however, call me to have more faith.

"You of little faith," he said, "why did you doubt?" (Matt. 14:31)

I praise you, God, for you promise to guide and take care of me. May I leave all my stubborn doubts behind and follow you. Amen.

Write down one of your doubts and throw away the paper as a sign of trusting your doubt to God.

The Great Storm Is Over   February 27

This morning the chorus of one of John McCutcheon's songs keeps running through my head:

Hallelujah, the great storm is over;
Lift up your wings and fly.

I think of my friend Marge, who died of cancer two years ago, and I still miss her. But when I think about the great storm she endured at the end of her life, it's comforting to know she's now free from this world. I like to think about her now as healthy enough to lift her wings and fly to God.

He will wipe every tear from their eyes. There will be no more death or mourning or crying or pain, for the old order of things has passed away. (Rev. 21:4)

God, thank you for receiving Marge and restoring her to new health. Comfort us who are left behind in our loss, with the reminder of her presence with you. Amen.

Remember a loved one whose great storm is over.

Having Fun with God   February 28

Becoming bogged down with my studies and work can take all the fun out of life. I think I have so much to do that I can't take a little time off to go to a party with my friends or play the piano or read a book or even do nothing just for fun.

I don't think God wants me to be that busy. If I'm always working or worrying about everything I have to do, God has to work overtime. I want God to give me strength to do my work and then also keep me from becoming too run-down with worry.

When I find myself constantly busy, it's time to give God and myself a break and go to a party together or take a walk. God likes to have fun with me too.

Come to me, all you who are weary and burdened, and I will give you rest. (Matt. 11:28)

Thank you, Savior, for your promise of giving me rest. I thank you that I can take time off with you to have fun. Amen.

Eat a favorite treat with God.

Teachers—Are They Human?

Teachers—who are they? They're good topics to discuss and laugh about with friends. They're something to be avoided when rules are broken. They're objects of resentment when they give homework the night of a ball game. They're receivers of many unkind comments. But most important and sometimes least remembered, they're people.

After learning to know some of my teachers as friends instead of as dictators, I have been able to understand them better. Surprisingly enough, they have the same hurts, worries, and cares as every other human. Admittedly, to some of them teaching is only a job, but to most it's a job in which they can help students in the best way they know how. What other job requires working far into the night on the next day's lesson plans or correcting papers? Teachers are some of the most dedicated people I know. I'm sure many times they don't feel like grading my papers any more than I feel like writing them, but they do it to help me, even if I don't always appreciate it. They deserve more praise than is given to them.

Think highly of them and give them your whole-hearted love because they are straining to help you. (1 Thess. 5:13 LB)

Thank you, Jesus, for all the people who have dedicated their lives to giving me a good education. Teach me to appreciate their work and not to take it for granted. Help me know each one as a person, not as a dictator. Amen.

Thank a teacher.

MICHAEL SILUK

Let There Be ...   March 1

In the beginning of creation God said, "Let there be light," and there was light. God said, "Let there be heavens and earth," and they appeared too.

In the beginning, whatever God commanded happened. But then people came and God gave them choices.

Now God wants peace, but people sometimes choose to be greedy. God wants joy, but people choose selfishness. God wants to do so much with my life—all I have to do is listen to God's voice. Then God can say, "Let there be helpfulness," and there will be.

When I wonder why God doesn't work miracles in my life as he did in Genesis, I have to ask myself if I'm not the one standing in the way.

Then God said, "Let there be light." And light appeared. (Gen. 1:3 LB)

Lord, let me be open to you. Work in my life and carry out your miracles through me. Amen.

What would God like to create in your life?

———◆———◆———◆———

Praise God   March 2

In recent experiences, I've found that it's easy to praise God when good things are happening. The difficult time to praise him is when disaster strikes. When studies are hard and don't seem to get done, when friends seem insensitive to my needs, when a disagreement has taken place—these are times when I ask, "Why?" I forget that God allows good and bad times alike but is always with me in all situations. Remembering that God alone knows the future and how all my present experiences are fitting in to make the best results,

I can trust and thank him for everything—even when it doesn't make sense to me.

For just as the sufferings of Christ flow over into our lives, so also through Christ our comfort overflows. (2 Cor. 1:5)

Lord, forgive me for times when I've complained about my hardships instead of praising you. May I be content in every situation, knowing that you are in control. Amen.

For what can you praise God?

Many Miracles   March 3

Two more rockets were blasted off into space, but this time I didn't watch. My great-grandparents would have watched this stupendous achievement spellbound—an achievement that has become almost commonplace for my generation.

Millions of miracles happen all around me every day, and I take them for granted. It has been said that the first time a thing occurs, it's called a miracle; later it becomes normal, and no attention is paid to it.

Worship and praise can become normal too. At special celebrations where everyone is singing and talking about God's amazing love, it's easy to become spiritually high and think Christianity is the best thing. The tough part is coming back home to the regular routine again.

Worship, however, doesn't have to become routine. Each day God performs many new miracles in my life. My job is to look for them and continue my praise every day.

Don't ever forget those wonderful days when you first learned about Christ. . . . Do not let this happy trust in the Lord die away, no matter what happens. (Heb. 10:32, 35 LB)

Your greatness, my Savior, is far beyond anything imaginable. I humbly thank you for giving me life, a rich supply of loving friends, and the biggest miracle of all, your Son, who died for me. Amen.

See life today as the miracle it is.

God Leads   March 4

"The will of God never leads you where the grace of God cannot keep you." Those words, on a poster, have come to have a lot of meaning in my life.

Being an impulsive kind of person, I often find myself in situations I can barely remember jumping into. I say I'll do a job and then feel overwhelmed and wonder how I can keep my commitment. I promise to be somewhere, and then other things crowd in and I wonder how everything will get done.

It's comforting to know that when I'm living in God's will, I won't be left stranded. My commitments and promises aren't made to be fulfilled on my own. I rest in the relief of God's grace—like sitting under a big tree on a hot day.

We live within the shadow of the Almighty, sheltered by the God who is above all gods. (Ps. 91:1 LB)

Thank you, Almighty God, for the knowledge that wherever your will leads me, your grace will also keep me. Amen.

Review your plans for the day ahead. Are they in God's will? You do not go alone!

The Light of the World   March 5

When light shines through a prism, it's amazing how many colors its rays reveal. On a sunny day the prism hanging in our living room window splashes at least twenty splotches of rainbow colors all over the room.

Jesus Christ is the Light of the World, yet many people haven't seen how beautiful that light is. Christ has many faces to be seen, and the only way that can be accomplished is through his followers. The important job of shining Christ's light in all its glory to those around us is a big task, and it belongs to each of us.

Don't let anyone look down on you because you are young, but set an example for the believers in speech, in life, in love, in faith and in purity. (1 Tim. 4:12)

Jesus, thank you for entrusting to me the job of being a prism for your light. Amen.

Splash your colors all over your corner of the world today.

Our Father   March 6

I watched a film during which we were all told to stand and repeat the Lord's Prayer together. After we said, "Our Father," we were stopped and told to sit down again.

The film went on to emphasize the fact that God is our Father and that makes us all brothers and sisters in him. All who stood and said, "Our Father," have the same Father, even though many of us didn't know each other. Thinking about everyone as being in one family makes each person seem special and worth learning to know. Even if I'd rather not be a sister to someone, I can't disown that person, because by having the same Father, we're in the same family.

But you are not to be called "Rabbi," for you have only one Master and you are all brothers. (Matt. 23:8)

Father, thank you for the sense of unity I have with those around me by knowing that because of you, we're all brothers and sisters. Amen.

Meditate on what "Our Father" means to you.

God as Our Mother   March 7

At the sound of the tiny infant's cry, his mother picked him up and put him to her breast. Without opening his eyes, the baby began to suck contentedly. He was too young to understand where the nourishment came from or even that he needed it, but his mother lovingly continued to give.

God, too, continuously meets our needs and provides nourishment for our lives, even when we're oblivious to where it comes from. And as with any child with its mother, our appreciation will grow as we become more aware of who God is for us.

How often I have longed to gather your children together, as a hen gathers her chicks under her wings. (Matt. 23:37)

God, like a mother with a child, you provide nourishment for me. Thank you, and help me to grow in my awareness of you. Amen.

Take a few minutes to imagine being a chick under the wing of God's care.

Growing Pains   March 8

Hurts, hurts, and more hurts. If I'm a Christian and God loves me so much, why am I allowed to hurt? I may ask this question often and may become bitter if I don't keep reminding myself why God allows hurts in my life.

Being a Christian doesn't mean my misfortunes will automatically disappear. God doesn't simply move into action every time I want a miracle performed.

Looking back, I can see how various hurts in my life have helped me. It's easier for me to understand what a friend is going through if I have already experienced a similar hurt. I can help people pull through rough times by sharing my experiences and encouraging them. Hurts can actually become blessings in this way.

If all Christians were shielded against hurts, we could no longer be sensitive to non-Christians, and communication with them would be lost.

Give thanks in all circumstances, for this is God's will for you in Christ Jesus. (I Thess. 5:18)

Equip me, O God, in any way you choose, to be a better servant for you, even if it means hurts. Grant me an attitude that seeks to find the good in everything, even if it takes a while. Amen.

Think of the hardest part of the past week. Can God use it for good?

———————— ••◆•• ————————

Listening to Christ   March 9

Prayer and communication with God is one of the most essential parts of the Christian life, but sometimes it becomes almost meaningless. Too often my prayers are a monologue—I talk but don't listen and thus don't give Christ a chance to talk to me.

I am often more eager to act and talk than to listen. I need to learn to listen, not only to others but also to Christ.

Prayer has at least two objectives: talking (or thinking) and listening. I must learn to spend more time listening.

And Samuel replied, "Yes, I'm listening." (I Sam. 3:10 LB)

Lord, forgive me when I talk too much. Teach me to listen to others and to you. Amen.

Listen to some relaxing music that helps you forget yourself and focus on Jesus.

Think   March 10

When I'm with friends, it's hard to remember that God gave me two ears and one mouth for a purpose—to listen twice as much as I talk.

Along with the urge to talk comes the tendency to talk about people who aren't around, and this can be bad if it is derogatory talk or gossip. A friend gave me a hint to help me with this problem, and it works if I stop long enough to *think* before making a comment about anyone.

T - Is it True?

H - Is it Honest?

I - Is it Important?

N - Is it Necessary?

K - Is it Kind?

If the answer to any of these five questions is no, then what I might have said isn't worth saying.

Beloved, do not grumble against one another, so that you may not be judged. (James 5:9 NRSV)

Dear Jesus, forgive me for the times I've spoken unkindly about a classmate. Help me to think before I talk. Amen.

Write THINK where you can see it all day.

Thy Will Be Done   March 11

Too often I find myself praying as if I want God's will to be changed, instead of praying, "Thy will be done." Jesus promises that our prayers will be heard if we ask anything according to God's will, but it's not always easy to know what that is. Sometimes we try to manipulate God or ask for others to be manipulated so that everything will turn out according to our will. Unless I'm consciously seeking God's will, it's easy to substitute my own selfish desires.

This is the confidence we have in approaching God: that if we ask anything according to his will, he hears us. (1 John 5:14)

Lord, keep me mindful of your will. Teach me to pray according to what you want and to be satisfied with that. Amen.

Thank God for the gifts of yesterday.

Your Will—My Desire   March 12

In looking for a summer job, I was faced with two options that seemed equally good. Each would clearly be a way of serving God. Although I knew I would enjoy the one much better than the other, I wanted most of all to do God's will.

In helping me decide, a friend said, "If you know God is okay with either one, do what you would most enjoy. God loves you and wants you to enjoy life, much like your mother wants you to have your favorite meal for your birthday!"

God saw all that he had made, and it was very good. (Gen. 1:31)

Thank you, God, for all the beauty you have created for me to enjoy. Help me to love you more deeply by accepting your love. Amen.

Pay attention to your desires. Are they from God?

Strength with Christ   March 13

Recently, I listened to a preacher tell a story to children. For an illustration he used a toothpick, a nail, and a rubber band. The toothpick, which the children were able to break in two with no problem, represented a person. The nail, which no one could even bend, represented God and the united body of believers. Then the preacher bound a toothpick to the nail with the rubber band, and the toothpick could no longer be bent or broken.

I am like a toothpick. Anything can happen if I stand alone, but when I'm united with Christ and other believers, I can't be broken.

We who are strong ought to bear with the failings of the weak and not to please ourselves. (Rom. 15:1)

Thank you, Savior, for being my strength to lean on. Amen.

Put a nail in your pocket and let it be a reminder of the strength God offers to you.

How to Be Perfectly Miserable

Some time ago I came across an article entitled "How to Be Perfectly Miserable." It opened my eyes to ways I was actually making myself miserable! Some of them are:

Think only about yourself.

Talk only about yourself.

Use "I" as often as possible.

Mirror yourself continually in the opinion of others.

Listen greedily to what people say of you.

Expect to be appreciated.

Be sensitive to slights. Never forget criticism.

Be suspicious, jealous and envious.

Trust nobody but yourself.

Insist on consideration and respect.

Demand agreement with your own views on everything.

Sulk if people are not grateful to you for favors.

Never forget a service you have rendered.

Be on the lookout for a good time for yourself, shirk your duties if you can.

Love yourself supremely, be selfish, and do as little as possible for others.

Love ... is not rude, it is not self-seeking, it is not easily angered, it keeps no record of wrongs. (1 Cor. 13:4–5)

Prevent me, Lord, from indulging in the selfishness that only makes me miserable. Amen.

Pick one phrase from the above list and practice its opposite today.

The Opposite of Love—Self

"The opposite of love is not hate, but self. The more of self the less we can love." Those words, written in our church bulletin, made me stop and think.

Amy Carmichael captured this thought in *If*, a book she wrote about love. "If I am afraid to speak the truth, lest I lose affection, or lest the one concerned should say, 'You do not understand,' or because I fear to lose my reputation for kindness; if I put my own good name before the other's highest good, then I know nothing of Calvary love."

Create in me a new, clean heart, O God, filled with clean thoughts and right desires. (Ps. 51:10 LB)

Lord, I share the prayer of the psalmist. Take away my old self and put your Spirit in its place. Amen.

How can you turn a selfish desire into giving love?

Impatience

March 16

A man confessed to his pastor, "I love God all right. My problem is that I don't love people."

When friends rub me the wrong way and I'm quick to react to what others say or do, then I know how immature I am in the Christian life. Impatience is sometimes excused as a sensitive spirit or nervousness, but if Christ can't be seen in my relationships to other people, practical Christianity is not present.

The test of patience is not how much I love God, but how much I love the people I come in contact with each day. That, in turn, is how much I love God. Patience, one fruit of the

Spirit, is cultivated and grown in my close relationships with others.

Love is patient, love is kind. (1 Cor. 13:4)

Lord, increase my patience in all my relationships, even when I don't agree with everyone. Amen.

Who do you find it hardest to love? Ask for the desire to love in new ways.

———— •• ——— •••• ——— •• ————

A *Spirit of* Pride   March 17

Becoming wrapped up in my own world of studying, working, friends, and fun happens too often, and it can be dangerous. It naturally makes what I do and think seem most important, and what others do is therefore of less consequence.

This kind of selfishness, which quickly becomes pride, puts aside the love I could give to others. Only in putting myself aside is it possible to love my brothers and sisters as Christ wants me to, having confidence in them and spending my time building them up instead of only building my own ego.

[Love] bears all things, believes all things, hopes all things, endures all things. (1 Cor. 13:7 NRSV)

Master, develop in me the kind of love that puts my own desires aside for the sake of others. Amen.

Think of a favor you would like to have done for you . . . and do it for another.

———— •• ——— •••• ——— •• ————

A Stubborn, Arguing Spirit

March 18

A girl was asked to play the piano for church one Sunday morning, but she refused, saying she wasn't good enough. After much coaxing from the choral director, friends, and family, she consented.

This same girl might have felt rejected if no one had asked her to play or encouraged her. The self wants to be coaxed when asked to do something but finds fault if it's not asked.

Love, on the other hand, tries to work for the good of all.

Work happily together. Don't try to act big. (Rom. 12:16 LB)

Savior, place in me the love that doesn't let stubbornness and a critical attitude take over. Thank you for your example of unconditional love. Amen.

Offer to share one of your gifts.

Fear

March 19

Fear of what others will think of me is also a mark of self-interest rather than love. I can remember many instances of not expressing my opinion, not doing something, or not going somewhere, because I was afraid of the disapproval of others.

I wonder if love was the lacking ingredient. If love is present in relationships, fear is cast out. Then I don't have to worry about what others are thinking of me nor waste my time judging them.

There is no fear in love. But perfect love drives out fear, because fear has to do with punishment. (1 John 4:18)

Lord, give me more of your love that casts out fear, so that I may live completely for you. Amen.

Write a love letter to yourself from God.

———•◦•≡•≡•◦•———

A *Spirit of Envy*   March 20

As I listened to the neighborhood gang of grade-school children arguing about who was the smartest, it was easy to see an envious spirit among them. This type of envy sometimes seems childish to teenagers or adults, but envy is often seen in us too, in quieter or more subtle ways.

Envy is present when an unpleasant feeling or thought is the first to enter my mind at a friend's success. Envy shows up when I speak of another's failings instead of his or her virtues. Envy is often prevalent within peer groups in which everyone would like the same position of importance. Real love is the only thing that can overcome envy.

Love . . . does not envy, it does not boast, it is not proud. (1 Cor. 13:4)

Thank you, Jesus, for your example of perfect love that rejoiced with the happiness of others. Create in me happiness for the success of my friends. Amen.

Be happy with someone.

———•◦•≡•≡•◦•———

Formality and Deadness

March 21

Formality and deadness, dryness and indifference in spiritual things arise in a life lived for self. When I think only of myself, the quest for ease, money, and the luxuries of life becomes the most important thing to me. Self-interest does not sacrifice; as long as I remain self-centered, no love can shine through.

Real spiritual vitality cannot break forth unless I put selfish desires aside and put others first.

Now that I, your Lord and Teacher, have washed your feet, you also should wash one another's feet. (John 13:14)

Lord, with your help I want to forget myself and give myself to others in love. Guide me in the exciting life with you. Amen.

Write your definition of love.

———————

Criticism Is Destructive

March 22

A girl in my class whom I didn't know well often told me my faults. Another person in my class, one of my closest friends, asked me to forgive him for bad feelings he had previously had toward me because of my actions. In both instances I had done wrong, but my reaction to one method of confrontation was the exact opposite of my reaction to the other.

When the girl made her accusations, I felt she was making them out of spite and jealousy. Instead of trying to correct my faults, I became angry from hurt.

On the other hand, my friend was confessing his own faults to me so we could have a better relationship. And that's exactly what happened. Although we didn't make a habit of telling each other our faults, this situation helped bring us closer in real Christian love.

That taught me a valuable lesson. It's not my duty as a Christian to constantly be telling others their faults, but to make sure I'm doing the best I can. Their enemies do a good enough job of letting them know their faults, without my helping.

Dear brothers, don't be too eager to tell others their faults, for we all make many mistakes. (James 3:1–2 LB)

Dear Lord, show me my own faults, and help me not to look for the faults of others. Amen.

Imagine the person of whom you are most critical being held in God's hands.

———————————

Jesus' Undeserved Love March 23

The last time I read Matthew 26, a new thought hit me. When Jesus went off by himself to pray before his death, he told his disciples to keep watch and pray with him, but they fell asleep *three times!* They were his best friends on earth, and they didn't even stay awake to pray with him when he was obviously filled with sorrow and would soon die!

I'm sure I do things that are just as disappointing to Christ. Sometimes I don't even deserve the status of "friend," and yet I have it. Jesus continues to love and care for each of us through all our unfaithfulness.

Then he said to them, "My soul is overwhelmed with sorrow to the point of death. Stay here and keep watch with me." (Matt. 26:38)

Thank you, Jesus, for loving me even though I don't deserve it. Amen.

Accept Jesus' gift of undeserved love.

Spiritual Disasters at Home

March 24

Statistics show that more than half the people killed in falls die in their own homes. The home, which should be one of the safest places, is especially dangerous. That's probably because when we are at home, we are relaxed and not watching for stumbling blocks.

The same is also true of spiritual disasters. My family has been the recipient of some of my worst displays of temper, selfishness, cruelty, jealousy, neglectfulness, and carelessness. When the people I'm with are the people I love the most, I have all the more reason to behave in a Christlike manner and be on my guard against stumbling blocks.

He will not permit the godly to slip or fall. (Ps. 55:22 LB)

Make me conscious, Jesus, of the need my family has to see your likeness in me. Amen.

Show a family member your love.

Mid-Year Blahs

March 25

The beginning and end of a race are the easiest to run. At the beginning, I'm fresh and eager to get going, and when the end is near, my spirits are revived to help me cross the finish line. The middle part is when I feel like quitting. I'm already worn out, and the distance to the finish line seems too great.

A school year is much the same. After a long summer vacation, my good intentions for studying hard this year are put to work.

But after a few months of this studious attitude, the mid-year blahs set in. The motives for studying hard aren't as clear any more. The work becomes boring, monotonous, and painful.

This is when having a long-term goal is helpful. Education is a means of making me into the best instrument possible for God to use in kingdom work. Since I want to make serving God my life goal, I must take advantage of all the training I'm receiving, so I will be better equipped to tackle the job God has waiting for me.

. . . they will run and not grow weary, they will walk and not be faint. (Isa. 40:31)

Lord, even through the rough mid-year blahs, help me to see purpose and meaning in my studies. Instill in me a determination to stick to my work and to do my best. Amen.

Pray for clarity of goals before each new task today.

———————◆◆——◆◆◆——◆◆———————

Idolatry?   March 26

We walk as pilgrims through the earth,
With empty hands, bereft and bare;
To gather wealth were little worth—
'Twould only burden life the more.
If men will go the way to death,
With them we will part company;
For God will give us all we need
To cover our necessity.

—Tersteegen

Just as God provided manna in the wilderness for the children of Israel each day, so he provides for me daily. If I store up possessions, I spoil the gift, just as hoarded manna rotted. I also spoil my relationship with God. Possessions become a barrier between us when I don't see my need of God for my security and safety. The more I trust God, the less I need to trust in things.

Do not store up for yourselves treasures on earth, where moth and rust destroy, and where thieves break in and steal. . . . For where your treasure is, there your heart will be also. (Matt. 6:19, 21)

Lord, show me when I become too involved in my earthly possessions. Help me to keep my life as burden-free as possible. Amen.

Give a treasure away.

Breathing Jesus' Likeness

March 27

I watched a baby today. After breathing primarily through her nose for five months, she was trying to learn how to breathe through her mouth. She screeched as she sucked the air in and breathed out heavily to let it go. It was hard for her to make a conscious effort to breathe; she had to learn to breathe in a comfortable, relaxed way again.

Watching this baby gave me hope that it will become easier and easier for me to be like Jesus. The things I read about and practice in a disciplined way now, can hopefully become a way of life—as normal and gentle as breathing!

Let your gentleness be evident to all. The Lord is near. (Phil. 4:5)

Thank you, Jesus, for your nearness. Teach me to be more and more like you. Amen.

Imagine God's Spirit going in and out of you with each breath.

The Book   March 28

A few weeks ago when I was looking for something to do, I picked up my Bible and began to look it over as a whole book. What a variety of things to read!

I had thought some of our laws today are strict until I found the laws recorded for the Israelites in the book of Leviticus. The book of Psalms contains beautiful poetry and songs praising God—I have discovered that these psalms express my joy so well. The Old Testament books are full of stories and prophecies that are even now being fulfilled! The New Testament also contains stories, as well as being the guide for living the best life possible.

I find it exciting that the Bible, written long ago by people in a different culture, is as up-to-date and relevant to me as tonight's newspaper.

No one else can be compared with you. There isn't time to tell of all your wonderful deeds. (Ps. 40:5 LB)

O glorious God, I humbly thank you for your gift of the Bible. It is an inspiration to me today to read about the experiences of those who followed you in the past. Amen.

Read a commentary's comments on your favorite verse.

Growing Continuously March 29

I once heard someone compare the Christian's walk in life to that of a weight lifter. A weight lifter knows the discipline of continuous untiring effort. He doesn't expect to be able to lift as many pounds as someone who has been lifting weights longer than he has. Through continuous work, he becomes stronger and can lift more and more.

The Christian life is similar in many ways to that of a weight lifter. A newborn Christian cannot know as much as one who's been a follower of Christ for a longer time, but by studying the Scriptures and having fellowship with other Christians and with God, the new believer becomes stronger. Like a weight lifter in his discipline, I have to remember that continual communion is essential for growth in the Christian life.

Then he said to them all: "If any want to become my followers, let them deny themselves and take up their cross daily and follow me." (Luke 9:23 NRSV)

O Master, I give you all my life to use for your glory. Give me patience to be content where I am, but help me to always be searching for new truths. Amen.

Lift the balanced weights of contentment and discontentment.

The Value of a Smile March 30

It costs nothing but gives much.

It enriches those who receive without making poorer those who give.

It takes but a moment, but the memory of it sometimes lasts forever.

None are so rich or mighty that they can get along
without it.

And none are so poor but that they can be made rich by
it.

It creates happiness in a home, fosters good will in
business, and is the countersign of friendship.

It brings rest to the weary, cheer to the discouraged,
sunshine to the sad, and is nature's best antidote for
trouble.

It cannot be bought, begged, borrowed, or stolen, for it is
something that is of no value to anyone until it is
given away.

Some people are too tired to smile, so give them one of
your own—since no one needs a smile so much as
the one who has none to give.

**I shall again praise him for his wondrous help; he
will make me smile again, for he is my God! (Ps.
43:5 LB)**

*Thank you, Lord, for smiling on me. Remind me of the
importance of a simple smile when I see someone who especially
needs one. Amen.*

Bask in God's smile.

———————◆—◆—◆———————

Joyful Faces   # March 31

Robert Louis Stevenson said, "When you looked into my
mother's eyes, you knew as if He had told you why God sent
her into the world—it was to open the minds of all who
looked, to beautiful thought." His mother's face showed her
inner joy.

Faces can show not only joy but also worry, resentment,
or discontent. My attitudes and thoughts are displayed on my

face. In my youth I determine my facial expressions for the rest of my life. It's important to be joyful—visibly.

My soul glorifies the Lord and my spirit rejoices in God my Savior. (Luke 1:46–47)

Thank you, Lord, for giving me the gift of joy. May it show on my face as a witness for you. Amen.

Smile at a stranger.

Time Conservation April 1

April is a busy month: term papers, the class play, various school and youth group activities, and homework. So much to do, but never enough time it seems.

Nevertheless, last April a friend and I seemed to find time to get together for at least fifteen minutes every day to complain about how busy we were and to worry about when we would have time to do it all. Obviously we weren't making the best use of our time. There were more subtle ways I wasted time too, like sleeping in instead of spending a few minutes with God before I started my day.

Even in my busiest schedules, I find time to do the things I really want or need to do. God has given each of us the same number of hours per day. How I use my time is my responsibility.

You have made my days a few handbreadths, and my lifetime is as nothing in your sight. Surely everyone stands as a mere breath. (Ps. 39:5 NRSV)

Master, let me walk with you. When I get too busy, slow me down enough to sort out my priorities in how to use my time wisely. Amen.

Dedicate April to God's timing.

Walking the Narrow Path April 2

The Bible describes the road the Christian travels as narrow. Many distractions tempt me to leave the path, and dangers scare me, but when I can see Jesus going ahead with me every step of the way as my leader, I can have confidence.

When I take my eyes off Jesus and look down at the path instead, I am already in danger of going astray. I must always keep my eyes fixed on Jesus. That is the only way to stay on the narrow path.

But small is the gate and narrow the road that leads to life, and only a few find it. (Matt 7:14)

Lord, keep leading me along your narrow road, and by your grace, I will keep following. Amen.

Walk across the yard, looking at your feet. Try again, looking ahead to a focal point.

———————

Unselfish Love   April 3

I heard a story of a rich man who had bought a car for his brother. When the brother showed it to a friend, the friend said in awe, "I wish I could be a brother like that!" The expected reaction would have been "I wish I could *have* a brother like that!" This friend's unselfish love was strong.

When I tend to become too self-centered, this story is a good reminder of the kind of love Christ wants me to have for my brothers and sisters.

But Zacchaeus stood up and said to the Lord, "Look, Lord! Here and now I give half of my possessions to the poor." (Luke 19:8)

Lord, thank you for your witness of totally unselfish love. Teach me to walk in your footsteps of love. Amen.

Be the kind of friend you'd like to have today.

———————

True Communion with Christ
April 4

Sometimes I find myself doing things out of habit or to look good. I don't really do them out of a response to Christ's love, but I do them because I think I ought to. I need to remember that if I look good but have my back to God, I'm no better than those who don't even try to do good. My relationship with Christ is what counts. No showy religious put-on is going to keep me in the kingdom of heaven.

Blessed are the pure in heart, for they will see God. (Matt. 5:8)

Keep me close to you, Master, that I will always have my eyes on you and not just pretend to be your follower. Amen.

Get rid of the "shoulds" in your life.

Self-Acceptance
April 5

I have heard that the definition of humility is always putting oneself below the other person. If I think I'm the least important, however, I'm focusing my thoughts on myself, constantly comparing myself to others and coming out the loser.

A humble person, on the other hand, is one who hardly thinks about self at all. Humility rejoices with others rather than being obsessed with one's own success or failure.

In the gospel of Matthew, Jesus says that we are to love our neighbor as much as we love ourselves. If I love myself too much and always put my own interests before those of others, then I'm wrong. But it's also impossible to follow this commandment if I don't love myself.

Love your neighbor as yourself. (Matt. 22:39)

Loving Father, guide me in your way of humility in such a way that I will not feel I'm worth less than my brother or sister. Instill in me the knowledge that we're all the same in your sight. Amen.

Say "I love you" to yourself.

Light a Candle   April 6

I once read this intriguing statement: "It is better to light one candle than to curse the darkness." I felt as if it was addressed directly to me. I had just had the kind of day where I came closer to cursing the darkness than to lighting a candle.

When I concentrate on how bad things are, it's impossible to see any brightness. Only when I light a candle by thinking about everything I have to be thankful for, or by brightening someone else's day, will the darkness disappear.

You are the light of the world. (Matt. 5:14)

Thank you, Lord, for your reminder to light a candle for you. May I always remember to do that instead of cursing the darkness. Amen.

Focus on a lit candle as you pray.

Death or Life?   April 7

Death is a subject we are all familiar with, whether or not it has touched the lives of those close to us. It's hard to see death as a part of life, but for a Christian that is what death is. It isn't only an end but also a beginning, not only a parting but also a reunion. Dying isn't locking a door; it is going on to a better room. And best of all, death enables a person to be in closer communion with Christ. Life on earth is the waiting room to a huge and beautiful mansion being prepared for each of us.

Lord, help me to realize how brief my time on earth will be. Help me to know that I am here for but a moment more. (Ps. 39:4 LB)

Lord, when I begin to have doubts and fears about death, remind me of all the good that can be attained only through the death of my earthly body. Amen.

What is your image of heaven?

The Line of Life   April 8

In a group exercise we were each asked to draw a line representing the highs and lows of our experiences in life. My line was quite uneven. Sometimes it went fairly high, only to drop to some unpleasant low points. I really didn't want anyone to see my line. I was embarrassed to show how unstable I was. But to my surprise, everyone else had similar lines, and some were even more uneven!

After this experience I realized that everyone, being human, has good times, bad times, and in-between times. I also realized that that's not wrong; it makes life interesting and exciting. If I didn't have discouraging times, I wouldn't be able to appreciate the good times as much. The important thing to remember is that no matter what kind of mood I'm in, God is with me and wants to hear how I'm feeling.

Give your burdens to the Lord. He will carry them. (Ps. 55:22 LB)

Thank you, Jesus for going with me through each mood and helping me to make the best of every situation. Your presence is comforting. Amen.

Draw a line representing your life's experiences.

―――――••――••――――――

A Time to Risk   April 9

A lobster must shed its old shell many times in order to grow. After each shedding, it is completely defenseless until the new shell forms.

A similar risk is present when people change. Any change produces uncertainty. But without the uncertainty, no change or opportunities are available. Like the lobster, I must be willing to take the risk of vulnerability as the price for growth.

Be strong and courageous. Do not be terrified; do not be discouraged, for the Lord your God will be with you wherever you go. (Josh. 1:9)

Remind me, Lord, of your continuous watch over me. I know that with you I'll never be defenseless. Amen.

What old shell are you shedding?

―――――••――••――――――

Victory Over
Temptation   April 10

In 1 Corinthians, Paul warns against idol worship. At first glance that's an easy verse to accept—it can't be so hard to follow. But maybe I do have idols!

Spending money on things I want but don't really need, instead of letting God use my money, can be idol worship. Going on a shopping trip when I'm not looking for anything special is my downfall. I usually seem to find something that would be nice to have in my room, a good bargain on an item I've *always* wanted, or something beautiful I might be able to use some day. It's hard to pass up things I'd like to have, even if I don't need them.

But time, money, or anything I think of before God, is an idol. Only Christ can help me overcome this love for things.

No testing has overtaken you that is not common to everyone. God is faithful, and he will not let you be tested beyond your strength, but with the testing he will also provide the way out so that you may be able to endure it. (1 Cor. 10:13 NRSV)

Thank you, God, for the promise that you will help me in all my temptations. Thank you, too, for the assurance that you won't let me be tempted with more than I can take. Amen.

Go to a store and concentrate on the wonder of all the things available that you don't need!

———————

Love Shares   April 11

Susan Polis Schutz wrote the following thought for a greeting card:

Your heart is my heart;
Your truth is my truth;
Your feeling is my feeling;
But the real strength of our love,
Is that we share rather than control
Each other's lives.

True love is not possessive. The only way I can really love is to accept another person as she is and allow her to make her own decisions. When I give each relationship to God, I can learn to share another's life without feeling the need to control it.

I know whom I have believed, and am convinced that he is able to guard what I have entrusted to him for that day. (2 Tim. 1:12)

Thank you, God for your perfect love. Give me more of your loving Spirit as I seek to share rather than control others' lives. Amen.

Write Schutz's poem for a friend.

I Need God   April 12

A friend told me how God continually shows him weaknesses in his life just when he begins to feel that he's on top of everything. He related how this humbles him to see his need of God once again.

Since that time, I've noticed God working the same way in my life. When I become self-confident, it's easy to forget God, but it's not usually long before I'm crying out to God again for help. I need to remind myself that anything I achieve is through Christ's power and not my own.

And don't think you know it all! (Rom. 12:16 LB)

Forgive me, Jesus, when I forget you. Give me weakness to keep me mindful of my need for you. Amen.

Tell Jesus about one of your weaknesses.

Horizons of Love   April 13

Looking out across the land at the wide horizon is a peaceful experience for me. It reminds me of God's love. Whenever I go to one horizon, another lies ahead. There will always be another horizon, wherever I go, just as God's love will always surround me.

That's the kind of love Christians are told to have for each other as well. A love that is always present. A love that has no end. A love that holds up no matter what happens. A love that doesn't disappear with unpleasant circumstances. A love that is peaceful and beautiful forever.

If you love those who love you, what reward will you get? Are not even the tax collectors doing that? . . . Be perfect, therefore, as your heavenly Father is perfect. (Matt. 5:46, 48)

Thank you, God for showing me how infinite your love is. Give me the same love for all my brothers and sisters. Amen.

Meditate on the horizon.

Listen in Silence   April 14

It's a misty evening as the rain falls softly. The sun has been down for a while, but it's still light enough to see a little. That's my favorite setting for a quiet walk and talk alone with God.

Being with others is one of my favorite things, but in all the activity, sometimes I forget the necessity of being alone with God. I wonder if God sometimes feels like telling me to slow down, be quiet, and just listen for a while. But God patiently waits for me to realize it on my own and is waiting for me when I'm ready.

Being silent and listening to God and creation is rewarding. It's amazing how many different sounds can be heard. Above all, it's amazing what God has to tell me when I become still and am willing to listen.

Stand silent! Know that I am God! (Ps. 46:10 LB)

Thank you, God, for being so patient with me, one of your creatures who sometimes doesn't even stop to listen to her Creator. You're so wonderful—I want to be with you forever. Amen.

Spend time in a spot where you find it easiest to listen.

———◆—————◆———

The Right Train? April 15

I see life as two trains, with everyone in one or the other. The trains are going in opposite directions, and each person may choose which one to ride. No one is at a standstill. Each person must be going in one of the two directions.

God's train doesn't have as many seats, but the scenery is better. It's harder to hang on to, but when the destination is kept in sight, the extra effort is worth it. The beautiful fact is that God always welcomes new passengers, and he loves them as if they'd been on board the whole time. Why would I ever want to be on the train going away from God?

For I did not come to judge the world, but to save it. (John 12:47)

Lord, I'm so glad I'm on your train. Thank you for reserving a seat for me. Amen.

What color describes the scenery on your ride today?

———◆—————◆———

Grow in the Lord April 16

Peanuts have a unique and interesting way of growing. When the blossoms have been pollinated, the shoots bend down and their tips go beneath the ground. The peanuts then grow underground to ripeness and become useful for many things.

I also look up first to God and then bow to Christ and other members of the body of Christ for my own growth. My usefulness develops out of my maturity and availability.

But grow in the grace and knowledge of our Lord and Savior Jesus Christ. (2 Peter 3:18)

O God, my Creator, thank you for teaching me how to be useful on earth. Amen.

Kneel to pray.

Do Thoughts Matter?   April 17

Recently I read, "Be careful what you think, what you listen to, what you do. It is placed forever in the memory." I know that what I listen to and what I do are important, but how about what I think? Is that just as crucial for living the best possible Christian life?

A few Sundays later I heard a sermon that pointed me to Philippians for the answer. Paul tells us there, in the name of Christ, what to think about. Since God has commanded me to control my thinking, he must also give me power to control it. Some things are difficult to keep out of my mind, but I know that with Jesus' help I can forget them. If I fill my thoughts with the things God commands me to think about, there's no room left for impure thoughts.

Finally, beloved, whatever is true, whatever is honorable, whatever is just, whatever is pure, whatever is pleasing, whatever is commendable, if there is any excellence and if there is anything worthy of praise, think about these things. (Phil. 4:8 NRSV)

Lord Jesus, I confess that I haven't done my best at keeping my thoughts pure. Forgive me and help me to start today to control my thinking for your sake. Amen.

Memorize the verse above.

———◆◆◆——

More on Thinking   April 18

Recently I read a saying that caused me to do more thinking on the importance of my thought life:

> *Sow a thought, and you reap an act;*
> *Sow an act, and you reap a habit;*
> *Sow a habit, and you reap a character;*
> *Sow a character, and you reap a destiny.*
>
> —Anonymous

My thoughts are crucial to the well-being of my spiritual life. What I think is what I eventually become.

Some time ago a preacher told us to think of every dirty word we knew of and then ask God to keep those words out of our minds. As I understand Christ, however, we are to overcome evil thoughts, not by constantly battling them, but by cultivating good thinking. We are to exert every mental effort to think about things that are good and pure.

Each area of life is so important for living totally for Christ that I must not think that this one part—my thought life—doesn't make any difference. It will determine my destiny.

Keep a close watch on all you do and think. (1 Tim. 4:16 LB)

Strengthen in me, Lord, the power to cultivate pure thoughts. Guide me in all phases of life that I may think only that which will be for your glory. Amen.

Make a list of ten beautiful words.

———◆◆◆——

Part of the Truth   April 19

The parable Buddha told of ten blind men and an elephant is interesting. Each of the blind men was asked to touch the elephant and report what he thought an elephant was like. An argument soon began because each man thought the part he touched was descriptive of the whole animal.

Buddha said that is how we view truth. Too often I think that the little bit of truth I know is the whole truth. But people who have different ideas from mine aren't necessarily wrong. They may just have a different part of the truth.

As an Indian sage said in a parable about mountain climbers: "You don't get the view from the foot of the mountain. It is only from the top that you see the whole picture."

For we know in part and we prophesy in part, but when perfection comes, the imperfect disappears. (1 Cor. 13:9–10)

Thank you for being patient with me, Lord, as I seek the truth. Give me patience and understanding for others' concepts of truth. Amen.

Listen to another without judgment.

Amen   April 20

Recently someone related to me an experience he had in praying with a friend. At the close of the prayer they didn't say "Amen," because they felt God was still with them. They didn't want to turn God off with a hasty "Amen."

Too many times a quick "Amen" finishes a prayer, signifying one task done and readiness to move on to something else. I have to be careful that my "Amen" doesn't stop my communication with Jesus but is an incentive to continue it.

Amen. Come, Lord Jesus. (Rev. 22:20)

I want you to be with me continually, Jesus. May my "Amen" be not one of finality, but one of beginning the experiences I have to share with you. Amen.

Tie a string around your finger as a reminder of Jesus' presence.

———— •◦——————◦• ————

Who Is God? April 21

Who is God?

That's the question I put before my friend. Is God a judge or a lover? Is God my defense attorney, or do I have to defend myself before God? Is God my mother or father, brother or sister? Does God desire action or contemplation?

And my friend said yes.

God *is* many things, and on different days, as my needs vary, I will relate to a different aspect of God. I can use my question, "Who is God?" to box God in or to let my view of God be expanded.

We give thanks to you, O God, we give thanks, for your Name is near. (Ps. 75:1)

God, my Judge, Brother, Defense, Mother, Lover, Sister, and Father, I thank you that you are all these and more to me. Amen.

Meditate on a new aspect of God for you.

———— •◦——————◦• ————

Bound by Love

Westwood Purkiser said, "We can walk in fellowship with God with wrong ideas in our heads, but not with wrong attitudes in our hearts."

I like that. I have many friends who don't share exactly my opinions on everything about our lives under Christ's lordship. I'm glad, though, that we can be brothers and sisters under the same God in spite of our differences. The most important thing is for each of us to be responding to God's love and what we believe God calls us to be. We are bound together by that love.

I am a companion of all who fear you, of those who keep your precepts. (Ps. 119:63 NRSV)

Thank you, God, for uniting me with your other followers because of our common commitment to you. Amen.

Look at a globe or world map and be aware of your feelings about people in other countries.

Make a Joyful Noise to the Lord

The high-school choir I was a member of combined with nine other school choirs once a year to sing together. These spine-tingling experiences are unforgettable, and I'm sure God enjoyed the music we made in worship as much as we did. It made me think of how grand and glorious it will be when we sing to our great God with all the angels of heaven.

I noticed, however, that some of the faces in the audience and choirs looked as if we were marching into the worst place possible instead of to Zion, the beautiful city of God. They didn't seem to comprehend the words, "Rise! Shine! Give

God the glory, children of the Lord," or "Clap your hands, all ye people."

Singing in church often lacks enthusiasm too. We can't possibly be understanding the words and at the same time look as though we're attending Christ's funeral rather than celebrating the resurrection. We all need to pay attention to the words we sing and let our faces reflect the message.

I will sing to the Lord as long as I live. I will praise God to my last breath! May he be pleased by all these thoughts about him, for he is the source of all my joy. (Ps. 104:33–34 LB)

"O, for a thousand tongues to sing my great Redeemer's praise, the glories of my God and King, the triumphs of his grace." Thank you for the tongue I have to use for you. Amen.

Sing your favorite song of praise.

Start Jumping   April 24

Some time ago in our Sunday morning service a man told a story about his daughter. She repeatedly asked him to put her on top of the refrigerator so she could jump. He did what she asked, but she never jumped.

He went on to relate this incident to his spiritual life. He repeatedly asks God to show him areas in his life that need to be worked on, but when God does show him, he's afraid to jump in and start working.

That was a challenge to me to start jumping for Christ— not only for my own good but also so others can see what Jesus means to me, and maybe the jumping will be contagious.

Remember, therefore, what you have received and heard; obey it, and repent. (Rev. 3:3)

Forgive me, Lord, for all the times you've said "Jump" and I've continued to sit still. Give me the courage to start the work you have for me. Amen.

Jump into your day.

Trust in God   April 25

Recently a group of us were visiting at the home of a friend for a weekend. Our friend also had a blind guest. The blind man didn't talk much, but I could tell he was listening closely to everything around him. I was not aware, however, how much he was learning. By the end of the first evening, he was able to tell what kind of a person each of us was, what color our eyes were, and how tall and heavy each person was. With few exceptions, he described each of us accurately.

It made me stop and think about how little I'm aware of how well God knows me. God is always watching with the special interest of love, asking only that I trust.

Many blessings are given to those who trust the Lord. (Ps. 40:4 LB)

Teach me Lord, to put my trust in you. Thank you for your protection even when I don't fully appreciate it. Amen.

Close your eyes and listen to the sounds.

Glorify Life in Christ   April 26

In the past few years I've listened to many speakers tell about their lives before they became Christians. Some spent their entire speeches telling all the horrible situations they had been involved in and warning against trying any of them.

It seemed to me that it would be more helpful to hear others tell about what Christ has done for them and the kind of rewarding lives they have had as a result. Instead of spending time telling about bad experiences, concentrating on the good can be uplifting.

Do not envy the violent and do not choose any of their ways. (Prov. 3:31 NRSV)

Dear Jesus, grant that I won't try to win others to you by showing them how awful life without you can be, but by letting them see how wonderful it is to live with you. Amen.

Tell a friend something good you appreciate about life.

The Time Is Now   April 27

Margaret Storm Jameson, an English novelist, once said, "Most of us spend fifty-eight minutes an hour living in the past with regret for lost joys, or shame for things badly done, or in a future which we either long for or dread."

That's a lot of time to think about things that don't have an effect on changing our circumstances now. Each minute is an unrepeated miracle.

Be very careful, then, how you live—not as unwise but as wise, making the most of every opportunity, because the days are evil. (Eph. 5:15–16)

Thank you, Lord, for each minute. May I make the most of each miracle for your glory. Amen.

Enjoy the present!

The Step of Faith   April 28

When I think of the story of Peter's attempt to walk on water, I remember that Peter began to sink because he didn't have enough faith. But I can also focus on the fact that Peter was the only one to make the attempt. All the other disciples stayed within the safety of the boat.

Peter took the step of faith, without stopping to consider the possible danger. I, too, need to step out in faith, as Peter did, when the Lord calls to me.

"Come," he said. Then Peter got down out of the boat, walked on the water and came toward Jesus. (Matt. 14:29)

Lord, thank you for Peter's example of faith. May I always be ready to answer your call with that kind of faith. Amen.

How is God calling you to step out of your "safe place"?

Judge Not   April 29

A friend once told me that before she became a follower of Jesus it was easier for her to accept others as they were. Now the temptation was to be critical of others if they didn't know or understand the things she was learning, and to think less of them.

Christ spent a lot of time with sinners, loving them. If I love as Christ loves, I will love others rather than look down on them for not knowing about his love or misunderstanding it. How else can they know his love?

Do not judge, or you too will be judged. (Matt. 7:1)

Thank you, Father, for your infinite love. Guide me in sharing it with an uncritical attitude with those around me. Amen.

Turn a criticism into love.

Prayer Power   April 30

After praying about something for a long time, one of my friends told me she had given up on God because she never got any answers. Sometimes I feel like giving up, too, but looking at my friend's situation helped me to better understand God's way of answering prayer.

Just because God doesn't answer all my prayers the way I want doesn't mean that he doesn't care about me. It probably shows that he cares more by giving me what will be the best for me in the end, even though I don't understand now.

Too often I want immediate action in response to my prayers, but God sometimes answers "no" or "not yet." The test of faith is in whether or not I'm willing to accept and thank God for answers I don't understand.

Don't be weary in prayer; keep at it; watch for God's answers and remember to be thankful when they come. (Col. 4:2 LB)

Listening God, grant to me the patience to wait for your answer and the power to accept it with thanksgiving if it's not exactly what I was hoping for. Amen.

End your prayers of request with thanksgiving.

CLEO FREELANCE PHOTO

Strength Through Problems

The following statement of Robert H. Schuller is an affirmation to be remembered with each new problem:

I will be a different person when this problem is past. I will be a wiser, stronger, more patient person; or I will be sour, cynical, bitter, disillusioned and angry. It all depends on what I do with this problem. Each problem can make me a better person or a worse person. It can bring me closer to God, or it can drive me away from God. It can build my faith, or it can shatter my faith. It all depends on my attitude. I intend to be a better person when this problem leaves me than I was when it met me.

Be joyful in hope, patient in affliction, faithful in prayer. (Rom. 12:12)

Lord, thank you for showing me that my attitude determines what my problems make of me. Guide me in handling them. Amen.

Commit yourself to learning the good from a situation in which you've been angry.

Trustworthy

Last year, through many FBI investigations, the police in a neighboring town were found guilty of numerous unsolved robberies.

This reminded me once again how unstable things on earth are. I can understand why anyone who didn't have the eternal hope of heaven to hold on to could become frightened by what's happening in the world. It makes me thankful to have Jesus as my personal Friend, who promises to take care of me even though nothing around me seems worth trusting.

Fear not, for I am with you. Do not be dismayed. I am your God. I will strengthen you; I will help you; I will uphold you with my victorious right hand. (Isa. 41:10 LB)

Dear Jesus, I don't know what I'd do without you! Life would be meaningless. Thank you for being with me always. Amen.

See or hear today's news with Jesus at your side.

———◆◆——◆◆——◆◆———

Discover Hidden Talents   May 3

All people have within themselves fantastic amounts of talent waiting to be used and developed. The sad thing is that we often fail to uncover these talents, keeping them hidden.

When I'm tempted to think God must have missed me when handing out talent, I can be reminded of the parable in Scripture in which three servants were each given a different number of talents. The two who received the most made good use of them and were given more according to their ability. The servant with one talent buried it, and it was taken from him.

God has given me talents, but unless I make good use of them, they will be worthless and won't produce anything for the kingdom. Maybe the people who seem to be blessed with many talents are merely making good use of the ones they have. Instead of being jealous, I can concentrate on discovering my own talents and developing them for God's glory.

His master replied, "Well done, good and faithful servant! You have been faithful with a few things; I

will put you in charge of many things. Come and share your master's happiness!" (Matt. 25:23)

Kind Giver of gifts, thank you for giving me talents. Forgive me for complaining about what I don't have instead of developing what I do have. Amen.

Work on developing one of your talents.

———— •• ◄━━━━► •• ————

Get Moving! May 4

When my brother and I had finally mastered the art of controlling a canoe, we were quite proud of ourselves. We could go fast, stop, or move in any direction. We also learned that it's easier to turn a canoe around when it's moving than when it's stopped.

My Christian life must keep moving too. If I'm at a standstill, God has a hard time changing my direction. Like paddlers in a canoe, God can more easily redirect my life when I'm moving.

To everyone who conquers and continues to do my works to the end, I will give authority over the nations. (Rev. 2:26 NRSV)

Direct my ways, O God, as I travel through the waters of life. Give me strength to keep moving. Amen.

Tell God whether or not you think you're moving ahead in your Christian life.

———— •• ◄━━━━► •• ————

Focus on Jesus May 5

At a park near our home, my favorite plaything was a huge wooden barrel. It lay on its side, and three people could comfortably stand upright in it. By walking forward, then running, we could make the barrel roll at a fairly good speed.

Sometimes it rolled so fast that we fell. A helpful technique we soon learned was to focus on something that was stable outside the barrel. By keeping our perspective in that way, we didn't become dizzy as quickly.

In life, it's easy for me to become upset with the turn of events that continually arise. At those times the best thing to do is to focus on Jesus as my stability, to keep me from becoming caught up in the whirl of activity.

Let us fix our eyes on Jesus, the author and perfecter of our faith. (Heb. 12:2)

Dear Jesus, thank you for being my stabilizer in a world that moves so fast. Grant me wisdom to keep my eyes on you. Amen.

Smell a flower and thank the Creator.

───────◆──────◆──────◆───────

Building Life with Christ
May 6

I remember when a new church was being built in our town a few years ago. It seemed like a long time before the framework was finished. The building process, however, was only the beginning of the church program. After the church was built, the people used the building to go on to many additional programs.

Life can be similar to the building process. God is the architect and contractor. Walls and rooms are added as I'm ready for them, but the building is never finished. I need to keep cooperating with God to build more and better programs into my life.

Being confident of this, that he who began a good work in you will carry it on to completion until the day of Christ Jesus. (Phil. 1:6)

I thank you, God, for being the perfect Architect. I am yours to shape and build in whatever ways you know to be best. Amen.

Draw your life as a building.

Concentration   May 7

Many times, during school terms especially, it becomes evident to me that my ability to concentrate is weak. It's easy to let my mind wander and become involved in something else before I'm finished with what I'm doing. Then I find that having a long-term goal to work toward helps my immediate concentration as well.

For example, homework can be boring and seem like a waste of time, but when I think of it as a necessary step in educating myself to become who God wants me to be, homework becomes more worthwhile to me.

The same concentration is necessary for growing in my Christian life. It's hard to be kind to people who are unkind to me, but when the rewards of Jesus' love are kept in sight, it is worthwhile.

[Look] to Jesus the pioneer and perfecter of our faith, who for the sake of the joy that was set before him endured the cross, disregarding its shame, and has taken his seat at the right hand of the throne of God. Consider him who endured such hostility against himself from sinners, so that you may not grow weary or lose heart. (Heb. 12:2–3 NRSV)

Be with me Jesus, as I live my life on earth in preparation for my life in heaven. Instill within me the long-term vision of everything I do. Amen.

How do today's activities fit your life goals?

I Shall Pass   May 8

Etienne de Grellet wrote a poem that is sometimes read at graduation ceremonies, but it's also a good reminder for every day:

> I shall pass through this world but once;
> Any good therefore that I can do,
> Or any kindness that I can show to any fellow creature,
> Let me do it now;
> Let me not deter or neglect it,
> For I shall not pass this way again.

Each day is new. It will last twenty-four hours, and then it will be gone forever. Let us rejoice in the present moment.

Satisfy us in our earliest youth with your loving-kindness, giving us constant joy to the end of our lives. (Ps. 90:14 LB)

Thank you, Lord, for each new day. Help me to spend each one in a way that will be pleasing to you. Amen.

At the beginning of the day, thank God for what is to come. At the end, give thanks for what has been.

The River of Life   May 9

As I sat on the bank of a river winding through the Virginia mountains, I saw the water as symbolizing my life.

Like the water that flows continually even though it doesn't know its destination or what's around the next bend, I can't see far ahead in my life. I have to trust God to guide my path.

The rapids and falls in the river are like the rough areas in my life. When I'm faced with rough situations, they sometimes look unbearable. But when seen as part of the whole, they add beauty and sparkle to my life.

Inlets of water along the shore, at a standstill, had collected scum and debris. Again, I compared them to my life. If I don't keep moving along God's path, my life will get cluttered. The river of life is too exciting to refuse its flow.

And whatever you do, whether in word or deed, do it all in the name of the Lord Jesus, giving thanks to God the Father through him. (Col. 3:17)

Thank you, Lord, for controlling the flow of my life. Teach me to follow even when I don't know what is waiting around the next bend. Amen.

Be aware of the cycle of life as you drink today.

Enjoying the Mystery   May 10

High-school days can be the beginning of an entire life spent feeling uneasy about the future. Even though sometimes I can't wait to graduate, school provides a certain security. A whole new world and many new experiences await the graduate, and these can be scary or exciting, depending on how we view life.

Sometimes I wish I could look into my future and see what I'll be doing in a few months or years. Then I could simply make those decisions that would bring about that future without having to weigh all the pros and cons of each situation.

That might be easier, but it would be much less exciting. If I knew about some of the good things that await me, I might get bored with life now. Or I might not be as eager to go on with life if I knew some of the disappointments ahead.

God has chosen to keep my future a mystery to me and lead me one step at a time. Enjoying each new revelation to its fullest is the most rewarding way to live.

Since the Lord is directing our steps, why try to understand everything that happens along the way? (Prov. 20:24 LB)

Eternal God, it's comforting to know that you hold my life in your hands. Thank you for guiding my decisions. Amen.

Hug a friend.

Savor the Earth   May 11

It takes 7,500 trees to print the Sunday edition of the *New York Times*. One four-foot stack of newspapers, recycled, will save a tree.

Adam and Eve in the garden of Eden doubtlessly envisioned the resources of their world going on without end. Today, however, we know that these resources can be depleted unless we learn better ways of caring for our "home." We need to listen for innovative ways to conserve our resources and pray for fresh energy to make all our ways of life glorify God.

The LORD God took the man and put him in the Garden of Eden to work it and take care of it. (Gen. 2:15)

Creator God, thank you for this beautiful world in which we live. Teach me to live responsibly. Amen.

Hug a tree.

Jesus as the Guide May 12

A family decided to go on a camping trip. They spent many weeks making plans and getting ready for it. The day of departure finally arrived, but they couldn't go until they found a map they had lost.

Life without Jesus as guide is much the same. I can spend a lot of time talking, reading, and thinking about the journey; but nothing is of value unless I start moving with the commands of Jesus to guide me.

I am but a pilgrim here on earth: how I need a map—and your commands are my chart and guide. I long for your instructions more than I can tell. (Ps. 119:19–20 LB)

"Guide me, O thou great Jehovah, pilgrim through this barren land; I am weak, but thou art mighty; hold me with thy powerful hand." Amen.

Study a map of where you live, recognizing how God leads you along those roads.

Open Up to Love May 13

When the first guy I really cared about suddenly dropped me, I was crushed and for a long time refused to trust anyone. To share deeply of my feelings again was too great a risk. I felt that if I didn't really love a person, then when that person left, the hurt wouldn't be as deep and hard to deal with.

Some time later at a youth rally the speaker was talking about relationships. He said that hurt is as much a part of life as joy, love, and other emotions, if not more. If we don't leave ourselves open for occasional hurts, we won't be able to be loved either.

I realized that by protecting myself from hurt, I had also closed myself to the love of my friends. I had many friendships, but not on a deep, personal, sharing level. I soon found that life can have a much richer meaning when I'm willing to open my true self to others. It's scary but well worth it!

... and to know this love that surpasses knowledge—that you may be filled to the measure of all the fullness of God. (Eph. 3:19)

Lord, thank you for showing me how rich the joys of life can be when I become willing to let others know the real me. Amen.

Write God a thank-you note for some of the people who love you.

Report for Duty   May 14

While listening to a sermon by David Seamans, a professor at Asbury College in Kentucky, I was struck by the following statement: "Don't give God instructions—just report for duty." I realized that I'm often guilty of going to God for instructions after I've already decided what I want. Then I ask for God's approval of my plans. A more obedient way to live is to ask God for direction in making my plans. Then I'm not only assured of walking in Jesus' footsteps, but I also don't have to travel alone.

So you also, when you have done everything you were told to do, should say, "We are unworthy servants; we have only done our duty." (Luke 17:10)

Lord, I want to report for duty today and every day. Forgive me for the times I've given instructions instead of asking for them. Amen.

Ask God for the gift of listening.

Arguing   May 15

On a trip our class took to Boston, I spent an evening at the Boston Commons. It is a park where people gather to talk about anything they want to. If anyone disagrees, they argue openly. Soon a small crowd gathers around to listen, and some join in.

After some observation, I noticed that even though these people might have believed what they were saying, they seemed to be arguing for the enjoyment of arguing! It was a form of entertainment, and it didn't matter with whom anyone was arguing.

It made me wonder what Jesus would do if he were in that situation; I didn't think he'd be participating. It also reminded me of the many times I have argued about insignificant matters. By observing others, I realized how silly my own arguments must have looked to others.

Do everything without complaining or arguing. (Phil. 2:14)

Lord, too often I find myself caught in the trap of arguing. Grant that I will act in a Christlike manner instead. Amen.

Pray for a person with whom you find it easy to argue.

Living the Notes   May 16

A friend of mine thought of an analogy in which he compared singing to living with God. God is like my diaphragm, from which I need constant support to sing. When the notes rise, I need an extra push, just as I need extra strength from God when times become hard. To produce the best musical sound, the vocal chords must be kept free, not tightened. So I too must remain free to let God play the tunes of my life. To produce the right intonation of holiness God must be my support in every beat and measure of my life.

Holiness is forever the keynote of your reign. (Ps. 93:5 LB)

Thank you, God, for your support in hitting the high, low, and in-between notes of my life. Keep playing your song in me. Amen.

Sing a song of praise to God.

———————

Spring of Life   May 17

Spring is the time for plowing under the old sod and starting anew. It's a time to go barefoot and walk in the rain, a time to chase butterflies and explore new places. Spring, bringing a fresh smell and excitement in the air, is just waiting to waken the world to a glorious awareness of being alive.

Youth is the springtime of life. It is the time for sowing seeds that will be harvested later in life. Acts of beauty will produce good fruit. Seeds of discord will yield bad fruit. Now is the time to decide what kind of fruit I want my life to bring forth.

Flee the evil desires of youth, and pursue righteousness, faith, love and peace, along with those who call on the Lord out of a pure heart. (2 Tim. 2:22)

Thank you, loving Father, for the spring of my life. Guide me in sowing seeds for the fruit you want to produce in me. Amen.

Go for a walk, enjoying spring—your own and nature's.

———◆———◆———◆———

Inferiority Complex　　　May 18

Everyone knows what it is to have an inferiority complex, and everyone probably has one in some area. I often feel so alone in having one, but I'm also convinced it's normal.

It begins with the self-image I develop in my mind. To a large extent this picture I have of myself affects how I look, talk, and act. Like everyone else, I know what it's like to fail at something, and I know that failure can badly damage my self-confidence. It often tends to make me afraid to try again because I'm afraid of repeated failure or of what others will think of me. I'd rather hide in a hole.

Since inferiority complexes can be crippling, it is important to know how to get rid of them. First, I have to be honest with myself. Pretending I'm not interested in something or being too busy are excuses I can make for not trying.

I also have to change the picture I have of myself. Looking at myself as God sees me is a start. God loves me just as much as he loves the person to whom I'm tempted to feel inferior. Then I can recognize that God gives me strength that I don't have on my own.

I can do everything through him who gives me strength. (Phil. 4:13)

When I feel inferior to others, God of my strength, let me be reminded of your ever-present love for me. With your help, I can do all things. Thank you. Amen.

Look in a mirror and see yourself as God sees you.

———◆———◆———◆———

Handling Victory May 19

Yesterday I thought about overcoming defeat, but then I realized that victory can be just as hard to handle. When I finally have the verse ingrained in me that says, "I can do everything through Christ" (Phil. 4:13), then I can think of God and myself as partners. Danger begins, however, after I gain victory. It becomes easy to leave God out and change from having confidence in God to having confidence in myself.

A superiority complex and an inferiority complex are opposite extremes of the same frame of mind. I ask God for help and then take credit for what happens. I wouldn't like a friend doing that to me. These two verses must go together: "I can do everything through Christ" and "Apart from me you can do nothing" (John 15:5). Knowing how good the feeling of victory or accomplishment is gives me a glimpse of how pleased God must be to receive the credit.

Don't be conceited, sure of your own wisdom. Instead, trust and reverence the Lord. (Prov. 3:7 LB)

Lord, may I always give you the credit for things we do together. I know that without you I can do nothing. Amen.

Write a thank-you note to Jesus for the times you've felt good about yourself.

Prayer Power May 20

A study of the four gospels shows how prayer was the underlying vein of Christ's whole ministry. He lived, healed, taught, raised the dead, fed, and evangelized—all by prayer. He even died praying.

In the complexity of life, I tend to plan everything carefully, taking as many shortcuts as possible, and my prayer relationship with God is often one thing that gets cut short. I will be of little use to Christ, however, unless I learn to pray and witness as he taught his disciples. Just as he was given no other way, neither am I given any other way.

This, then, is how you should pray: "Our Father in heaven, hallowed be your name. . . ." (Matt. 6:9)

Keep me mindful, Lord, of the fact that prayer is necessary to being your disciple and that no shortcuts are available. Amen.

Pray the Lord's Prayer slowly.

———————

Give Me Only Your Love and Your Grace   May 21

*Take Lord, receive all I have and possess—
my memory, understanding, my entire will.
Give me only your love and your grace;
that's enough for me.*

These beautiful words of a song written by John Foley provoke a yearning within me. I want to pray them and really mean it, and yet the human part of me wants to hang on. I fear the unknown of giving up all that I have.

When I think about God's love and grace, however, I realize I have nothing apart from what God has given anyway. Maybe returning it all to God is my way of saying, "Thank you; let me never take these precious gifts for granted."

Every good and perfect gift is from above. (James 1:17)

Give me the grace, Lord, to live in your love and grace alone. Amen.

Pray as much of John Foley's prayer as possible.

The Beauty of a
Sunrise   May 22

Early one morning I climbed a hill with a few of my friends to watch the sunrise. Since it was the first time I would witness this exciting event there, I didn't know exactly what to expect. The sky was light for at least an hour before the sun first appeared over a distant mountain. Then it quickly rose into full view within a few minutes.

Seeing the sunrise reminded me of God's presence in my life. Sometimes it's more visible than other times, but it's always there. It made me hope that I can be an instrument for God's kindness as fresh and dependable every day as the sun, so others can experience and know his kindness too.

Every morning tell him, "Thank you for your kindness," and every evening rejoice in all his faithfulness. (Ps. 92:2 LB)

Thank you, Creator, for the reminder of your presence in the beauty of a sunrise. May I always serve you by letting your love shine through me. Amen.

Soak in the sunshine.

Prayer in Jesus' Name   May 23

I've heard people end their prayers with the phrase "in Jesus' name," and I say it often myself. But until recently I didn't understand the meaning behind the phrase.

In reading through a few commentaries on the gospel of John, I found that names in Bible times had meaning; they were not simply spoken syllables. A person's name stood for that person's entire being—manners, personality, beliefs, actions, and thoughts. When I pray or praise in Jesus' name, I'm relating to the person of Jesus, not merely to the five-letter word.

I will cause your name to be honored in all generations; the nations of the earth will praise you forever. (Ps. 45:17 LB)

Jesus, thank you that I have more than a name to worship. Thank you for all that you are to me. Amen.

Write down at least five things Jesus is to you.

Good-Byes   May 24

I have a hard time saying good-bye to people. I almost wish sometimes that I wouldn't become so close to the people I know I'll have to leave; then it wouldn't hurt so much to say good-bye. But looking back on the beauty of those friendships, I wouldn't want to give that up to escape the pain of parting either.

Life is a continual process of meeting people and leaving them, but no friendship is ever lost. Each friend becomes a part of me, and I become a part of him or her. Instead of complaining that I must leave friends, I should thank God for the time we were together. Then I can go on to make new friends and enjoy the immediate experiences of each new day and be thankful for who I'm becoming because of them.

Lord, when doubts fill my mind, when my heart is in turmoil, quiet me and give me renewed hope and cheer. (Ps. 94:19 LB)

Thank you, greatest Friend, for the many beautiful friends you've brought into my life. Thank you for helping me see the beauty of friendship even when sometimes I have to say good-bye. Amen.

Deepen a friendship.

God Is in Control   May 25

Out of the darkness
Shall come dawn.
Out of our striving
Shall come peace.
Not by our power
But by the power of God.

I copied these words from a poster one of my friends had hanging on her door. Every time I read them, I'm reminded of the peace and rest that God gives. In a world that looks hopeless, I'm glad I'm in the hands of God, who has control of everything. By God's power my efforts are rewarded.

Make every effort to keep the unity of the Spirit through the bond of peace. (Eph. 4:3)

My God, I'm thankful that I don't have to struggle through darkness on my own power. Continue to be my strength. Amen.

Spread God's light to one who's sad today.

Storms of Life   May 26

Storms, with thunder loud enough to make the windows rattle and lightning bright enough to light up an entire landscape, can be scary. Last summer we had a storm like that, and it felt as though the end of the world was near: one more crack, it seemed, and the earth would split into pieces.

It made me think of the God who had control of all that chaos. God's power *made* the immense power of the storm, which, in itself, was incomprehensible to me. Having God as my personal Friend, I don't have to worry about big thunderstorms and all the other things in life that seem threatening. I have security in knowing that the storms in my life are nothing compared to the power Christ has to help me overcome them.

Though the earth shakes and all its people live in turmoil, yet its pillars are firm, for I have set them in place! (Ps. 75:3 LB)

Thank you, Lord, for being my personal Friend even though I'm sometimes ungrateful and I don't deserve your love. Thank you for your great power that helps me through the storms of life. Amen.

What pillars does Christ provide for your life?

Blowing in the Wind   May 27

Last summer during a storm, an old, dead branch was blown out of the maple tree beside our house. That saved us the bother of cutting it off, so we were glad.

Strong winds in life can be of use too. Sometimes they do what nothing else can do—blow down dead branches that have detracted from the tree's appearance. Instead of trying to stop the wind from blowing, I should be aware of what needs to be blown out of my life and rejoice when it happens.

But because of his great love for us, God, who is rich in mercy, made us alive with Christ even when we were dead in transgressions—it is by grace you have been saved. (Eph. 2:4–5)

Keep the winds blowing in my life, Lord, to help clear away all that is hindering my appearance in your sight. Amen.

Pay attention to the wind as a gift from God.

Work for God   May 28

Many people enjoy watching football games. While twenty-two tired people are working hard on the field, the stands are packed with spectators. They relate to the players but are uninvolved in the actual work of playing the game. The spectators may be in need of the exercise and are critical of everything the players do wrong, but they leave the action to the few who are willing to play.

Life is much the same. A majority of the Christians are content to sit back and watch a few do the work. Unless I get into action and join the team that's working for God, I can't expect to reap the benefits.

He said to them, "Go into all the world and preach the good news to all creation." (Mark 16:15)

Motivate me, God, to start working for you and not be content to be a spectator, watching others do your work alone. Amen.

Help make dinner.

Pain as Well as
Sunshine   May 29

All sunshine makes a desert. If you've ever been on a hot, dry desert, you were probably thankful for an occasional cool breeze or rain. Similarly in life, the happy, bright days are often preferred to the cloudy, rainy ones. But God, in mercy, knows that too much sunshine would dry us up, and so he provides all kinds of weather. I need to remember, when the clouds block out the sunshine, that every kind of weather is needed to produce the right climate for my growth.

Lord, grant us peace; for all we have and are has come from you. (Isa. 26:12 LB)

Thank you, Lord, for clouds as well as sunshine. Let me be content in having you as my weather regulator. Amen.

Take account of the climate of your soul.

———◆◆—◆▶—◆◆———

Frustration   May 30

The definition of frustration is "the blocking of the individual's progress toward a given goal or thwarting of the satisfaction of certain needs." The thing that strikes me in this is that frustration is caused when the *individual's* goals are blocked. Maybe I'm often frustrated needlessly because I make my own goals instead of asking first what God's goals are. God knows better than I what I can handle and how long it will take. Many times frustration can be eliminated when I'm willing to turn my goal-setting over to God.

A rebel's frustrations are heavier than sand and rocks. (Prov. 27:3 LB)

O God, you know the goals I can meet. I pray that I will leave that job totally up to you. Amen.

Ask God what the goals of your day are to be.

———◆◆—◆▶—◆◆———

Thorns or Roses

Seeing the roses bloom at the beginning of summer reminds me of a poster that said, "You can complain because rose bushes have thorns, or rejoice because thorn bushes have roses."

The truth of that statement can be broadened to apply to much of life. When I'm willing to look long enough, I can usually find something for which to be thankful. What looks bad at first glance may have value if it's seen from the right perspective.

You have done so much for me, O Lord. No wonder I am glad! (Ps. 92:4 LB)

Lord, teach me to look hard enough to find the good in things before I complain. Amen.

Smell a flower and be glad.

CLEO FREELANCE PHOTO

Judas   June 1

Little attention is given to Judas Iscariot except in relation to his betrayal of Jesus. Going beyond that fact, however, Judas is portrayed in other ways as well.

Like the other eleven disciples, Judas was with Jesus, helping him during his three years of ministry. He gave up his home and job to become a follower of Jesus. When Jesus said one of the twelve would betray him, none of them had any idea who it was, so Judas must not have done anything previously to make him seem guilty. After he betrayed Jesus, his grief was so deep that he couldn't face it. Judas is most remembered for the evil he committed, but he also must have loved Jesus.

When morning came, he called his disciples to him and chose twelve of them, whom he also designated apostles: Simon . . . and Judas Iscariot, who became a traitor. (Luke 6:13–14, 16)

Help me, Lord, not to prejudge other people even when the bad in them is most apparent. Help me to recognize that they have needs also. Amen.

Renew your New Year's resolutions.

Thomas   June 2

Thomas is another disciple we often remember with some disdain as the doubter. He seems somehow less faithful because he wouldn't believe in the risen Christ until he had seen for himself.

But Thomas, too, was one of the chosen twelve who gave up all he had to follow Jesus, and he was prepared to die with him. History also tells us that after Jesus' ascension, Thomas traveled to the East—possibly to Persia or India—to spread

Christianity under threats and persecution. His influence continues there today.

> **Then Thomas . . . said to the rest of the disciples, "Let us also go, that we may die with him." (John 11:16)**

> *Lord, help me, like Thomas, turn my doubts into an ever-stronger faith in action. Amen.*

Tell God about one of your doubts.

Motives and Actions   June 3

I remember the early spring days of my childhood when bright yellow dandelions covered our lawn and I picked huge handfuls to take proudly to Mother. Even though dandelions wouldn't have been my mother's favorite choice for a centerpiece, she always acted delighted as she helped me put all the short-stemmed weeds in a vase. It was my attitude of wanting to give her something that she appreciated, not necessarily the gift itself.

When I do a good deed, God also is more interested in the attitude of my heart than in what I do. It is important to live for Christ, but it doesn't amount to much unless my love and devotion to God are the motives behind my actions.

> **And this is my prayer: that your love may abound more and more in knowledge and depth of insight, so that you may be able to discern what is best and may be pure and blameless until the day of Christ. (Phil. 1:9–10)**

> *Lord, guide my actions that they will grow only out of the right attitude in my heart. May my love and devotion to you be the most important motivating force in my life. Amen.*

Examine your heart.

Finding Happiness

Happiness is a strange phenomenon. Sometimes it comes in abundance. At other times it's hidden so well I don't know if I'll ever find it again. Only by reaching out can I find true happiness, and then it's impossible to keep it for myself. The following way to happiness is of continual importance and I must remind myself of it every day:

Helpfulness to others
Always kind
Patience
Praise for God
Integrity within
Never envious
Establish friendly relationships
Speak only what is good and pure
Seek to love others more

Happy are those who long to be just and good, for they shall be completely satisfied. (Matt. 5:6 LB)

Thank you for happy times, Lord. Teach me to seek happiness for others, forgetting my own desires. Amen.

Make a new friend.

Stay in Tune

On one of our trips we were listening to a radio station from Pittsburgh. The farther from Pittsburgh we traveled, however, the less distinct the signal became. Finally communication was lost completely. They were still broadcasting at the radio station, but we were too far away to hear it.

In my life, Jesus is the radio station I tune in to. Jesus always remains available, and the closer I stay to him the better I hear his voice. If we seem too far apart at times, it's because I've moved. Jesus is constantly broadcasting. It's up to me to stay close enough to hear.

Neither height nor depth, nor anything else in all creation, will be able to separate us from the love of God that is in Christ Jesus our Lord. (Rom. 8:39)

Thank you, Jesus, for broadcasting your message continuously. Amen.

Let the radio waves you hear remind you of your communication with Jesus.

Foolish Questions? June 6

In a class where almost everyone was older and more experienced, I rarely asked questions. I was afraid the others would think my questions were foolish and insignificant. I either found the answers myself or asked someone after class.

When I think of God's infinite knowledge, many times greater than that of my wisest teacher, my problems and questions seem small. Nevertheless, another of God's indescribable traits is caring about every problem I have, no matter how small. God will never make me feel foolish for any question I ask. Nothing is too great or too small for God.

For the Lord grants wisdom! His every word is a treasure of knowledge and understanding. (Prov. 2:6 LB)

Thank you, Teacher, for your caring love, which enables me to ask anything of you with the confidence that you won't think it's stupid. Amen.

Tell God about all those little things that matter today.

Slow Down June 7

Done with my last exam of the school year, I kicked off my shoes and ran through the front lawn, enjoying my newly felt freedom. I was oblivious to all else, until . . . I stepped on the spot where a honeybee was working. It didn't waste any time letting me know it had been there first. That stopped me fast!

I heard God speaking to me through the sting of the bee. God seemed to be saying, "Enjoy your freedom, but be careful not to overstep your boundaries and hinder the freedom of another." It was a good reminder to me to remember others when the tendency is to think only of myself.

For I am not seeking my own good but the good of many, so that they may be saved. (1 Cor. 10:33)

Thank you, Giver of Freedom, for your small but unforgettable reminders to control my freedom if it interferes with someone else's. Amen.

Do another's task today.

Work for God June 8

One year when most of my friends were hunting summer jobs, I decided to stay home and help my parents. There was always plenty to do, but I was embarrassed when friends asked me what I was doing for the summer. Working at home sounded like play compared to working in a factory or restaurant, even though it wasn't.

Then I saw a beautiful picture of Jesus that impressed me. As others went about their daily tasks, he sat by the side, talking to the children. It showed me that I, too, should be willing to do what I know is right without worrying about what others will think of me. If I'm pleasing God with my work, the opinion of others doesn't matter.

Jesus said, "Let the little children come to me, and do not hinder them, for the kingdom of heaven belongs to such as these." (Matt. 19:14)

Give me satisfaction, O God, in doing what's right when others don't see everything. Thank you for your example of taking time out for the children, even though some of your friends thought it was a waste of time. Amen.

Who is your work pleasing?

Win by Losing   June 9

I asked God for strength, that I might achieve,
I was made weak, that I might learn humbly to obey . . .
I asked for health, that I might do greater things,
I was given infirmity, that I might do better things . . .
I asked for riches, that I might be happy.
I was given poverty, that I might be wise . . .
I asked for power, that I might have the praise of all,
I was given weakness, that I might feel the need of God . . .
I asked for all things, that I might enjoy life,
I was given life, that I might enjoy all things . . .
I got nothing that I asked for—but everything I had hoped for,
Almost despite myself, my unspoken prayers were answered.
I am among all people most richly blessed.

—Anonymous

I consider that our present sufferings are not worth comparing with the glory that will be revealed in us. (Rom. 8:18)

Christ, I thank you for giving me what you know I need even if I think I need something else. Amen.

Meditate on the lines above that touch you most deeply.

————————•———•—•—————•—

Exciting Changes   June 10

Wherever God's people are united in prayer, exciting changes are realized—changes in the life and spirit of the church, especially how it affects individuals. When God is allowed to enter and work in my life, radical changes are sometimes made.

A life of prayer becomes evident to each person it touches. Not only does prayer change individuals but it also creates a broader image to others that makes Christianity more attractive. People will more readily become a part of that which shows good fruit from what it preaches.

Ask and it will be given to you; seek and you will find; knock and the door will be opened to you. (Matt. 7:7)

Lord, make my times with you meaningful, and have your way in my life. May our relationship be one that others will see and desire as well. Amen.

Celebrate a change in your life.

————————•———•—•—————•—

Easter Is Every Day   June 11

Easter is a joyous time of celebrating the risen Savior. Every Easter Sunday I've gone to church and heard the Easter story through sermons, Sunday school lessons, and songs. At one particular Easter service, however, a poem was read that has stayed with me ever since. The poem said that Easter doesn't come only once a year but should be celebrated every day. The message of Christianity is that Christ rose from the dead for the sins of the world. Each day it is a new miracle.

He is not here; he has risen! (Luke 24:6)

Thank you, God, for the miracle of your Son's rising from the dead. May I be reminded that Easter isn't only one day in the spring, but every day of my life. Amen.

What difference has Christ's resurrection made in your life today?

No Barrier in Language
June 12

The science teacher took our class on a tour through the greenhouse. He had told us the day before about some of the plants and their names, but we couldn't picture their true beauty until we looked at them ourselves. We didn't need to know the names of the plants to enjoy them, but we did have to see or smell them.

In a time when many technical terms are used, it's easy to become confused with theological language. But whether or not I know the correct terminology, I can know the joy of Jesus' love and mercy. I need to see only the signs of Jesus' presence.

For Christ did not send me to baptize, but to preach the gospel—not with words of human wisdom, lest the cross of Christ be emptied of its power. (1 Cor. 1:17)

Thank you, Jesus, that I don't need to know big words to be able to understand your love. Be with me in conversing with others about you that I may do it simply enough that they too can understand. Amen.

Make Jesus' presence in you visible to another.

Reinforcing Praise June 13

Jo Coudert writes, "Praise reinforces good traits, criticism bad traits. Criticism produces defensiveness; and no one acts well out of defensiveness: one is rattled, shaken, and hurt. Criticism causes the personality to shrink, to be diminished, and not only the personality of its target but of its deliverers as well."

The next time I'm tempted to criticize another's bad traits, I should stop and ask myself whether or not I'm part of the cause of those traits by my lack of praise.

Share with God's people who are in need. (Rom. 12:13)

Teach me, Lord, to praise rather than criticize. Show me ways I can be of help—not another hindrance. Amen.

Reinforce another's goodness.

Everyone Is a Witness June 14

Many times we give the responsibility of witnessing to pastors. After all, that's their job. But, being the daughter of a pastor, I can testify to the fact that a pastor doesn't have more time than anyone else in the congregation. The pastor's job is to teach the people so they will be prepared to go out and share the gospel with their friends and neighbors. Spreading the gospel to the whole world is a bigger job than pastors can handle alone. Every follower of Christ is needed.

For we cannot help speaking about what we have seen and heard. (Acts 4:20)

Lord, grant that I will never be satisfied to leave to others the job you've given me, that of sharing your love. Amen.

Ask your pastor how you can help in the work of the church.

Witnessing Is Necessary   June 15

Not only is witnessing a part of every Christian's responsibility, as was suggested yesterday, but it is also essential to the Christian life. Frank Laubach writes, "It has often been said that we cannot keep Jesus unless we give him away. . . . Spiritual life is like electricity. No current passes through unless the wire is connected at the sending end as well as at the receiving end." The congregation has not finished its task until every member is involved in witnessing.

Never be lacking in zeal, but keep your spiritual fervor, serving the Lord. (Rom. 12:11)

I want to keep you, Jesus, by giving you away. May I always be a live wire for you. Amen.

Let lights you see remind you to keep your spiritual fervor alive!

Getting Along with Others   June 16

It has been said that all who want to be happy and successful must learn to get along with others. One step toward this is to be interested in others. I can win more friends in a month by being interested in them than in ten years by trying to get them interested in me.

Being interested in others may mean putting my own interests aside to become involved in theirs. It may mean doing my job and forgetting about receiving credit for it. It may also mean meeting criticism with good will and love. Whatever the means, showing interest in others will produce rich blessings.

Do not seek your own advantage, but that of the other. (1 Cor. 10:24 NRSV)

Teach me, O Lord, to forget myself in the interest of others. Amen.

Show an interest in a friend.

────────◆◆──◀━▶──◆◆────────

Getting Along with Myself

June 17

Another guide to a happy and successful life is the ability to get along with oneself. Conflicts with others usually stem from conflicts within ourselves. When children become fussy and irritable, it's often a sign that it's their bedtime. The same is true of adults. When I am easily bothered by others, it's a sign that I should look inside myself for the reason. When I settle my own inner disturbances, others tend to disturb me less.

Be joyful in hope, patient in affliction, faithful in prayer. (Rom. 12:12)

When I become irritated, Lord, remind me to look for the cause within myself—not to blame others. Amen.

Write down five things you appreciate about yourself.

────────◆◆──◀━▶──◆◆────────

Self-Forgiveness

June 18

I've often heard statistics about suicide: how many young people kill themselves, how many elderly kill themselves, how many persons with a chemical dependency lose hope and take their own lives, etc. Statistics are just that, however, until one knows a person behind them. The pain of suicide seared me deeply last year when a friend of mine killed himself. He was only nineteen years old but already felt that he had done too many terrible things and that God could never forgive him. The despair of that loneliness was too intense for him to live with.

God seems to intimate that no sin is worse than another and promises that all is gladly forgiven. But being human, we often have a hard time being convinced of that. We have a hard time understanding that we don't have to pay the penalty for what we've done. Forgiveness is a gift from God, but we also have to learn to forgive ourselves in order to accept it.

Praise the LORD, . . . who forgives all your sins and heals all your diseases, who redeems your life from the pit and crowns you with love and compassion. (Ps. 103:2–4)

Help me, O God, to accept a forgiveness I don't understand and to be able to forgive myself as well. Amen.

Tell Jesus about part of yourself you have a hard time forgiving.

Faith—Not Feeling   June 19

"But I don't *feel* like a Christian." Have you ever said that? I've felt that way at times and have heard similar statements from friends. It's really quite a normal feeling.

The times I don't feel like a Christian are the best times to form and strengthen my faith. I must keep going on the knowledge that I have life in Christ and that the good feelings will return. God is always faithful, waiting for my faith to return. As Joe Bayly said, "Don't forget in the darkness what you've learned in the light."

If we are faithless, he will remain faithful, for he cannot disown himself. (2 Tim. 2:13)

Thank you, Keeper of my soul, that I can know by faith that I am your child, even if the feelings aren't always present. Amen.

What's your favorite promise of God?

———————●—■—●———————

Begin in the Soul   June 20

A Chinese proverb says:

If there is right in the soul,
There will be beauty in the person;
If there is beauty in the person,
There will be harmony in the home;
If there is harmony in the home,
There will be order in the nation;
If there is order in the nation,
There will be peace in the world.

Too many times I look at things that seem impossible to change. I should, instead, begin with myself and see if everything is as it should be. Only then can I try to change other things.

Why do you see the speck in your neighbor's eye, but do not notice the log in your own eye? (Luke 6:41 NRSV)

Lord, teach me to set goals that I can handle before trying to change the whole world. Amen.

Assess your soul—is it right?

———————●—■—●———————

Learn to Say No   June 21

"Why did I let myself get into this? Why didn't I just tell them I couldn't do it?" Does that sound familiar? Many times I find myself asking these questions, but by then it's too late.

I once heard Arthur McPhee, a Mennonite pastor, speak on the subject of learning to say no. He said, "Your yeses don't mean much until you've learned to say no." I suddenly realized that it isn't the number of things I say yes to that's important, but what I say no to.

For each one should carry his own load. (Gal. 6:5)

Lord, guide me in knowing when to say yes and when to say no. Amen.

Do you need to say no to something for your own sanity?

Life's Greatest Aim   June 22

If asked what my greatest aim in life is, I might answer with a big dream, like to bring peace to the entire world. That goal would be nice, but I can't possibly accomplish it alone. In 1 Corinthians, Paul gives us a command from the Lord: love is to be our greatest aim. That sounds easy enough! I love everyone already.

But then he explains what God's love means, and when I think of specific people, it gets harder and harder to say I love them. "Love is patient, love is kind. It does not envy." Wow! It's tough not to wish I could live in a house like the one the neighbors have, or dress like my friend. "It is not proud. It is not rude, it is not self-seeking." I guess I wasn't being very loving yesterday when my sister had to wash the dishes alone because I was reading a good book. "It is not easily angered, it keeps no record of wrongs." But, Lord, how can I love that guy who always makes me feel stupid in English class?

I can't love—alone. By my own power I can't love everyone, but through Christ everything is possible. God can help me love people who seemed unlovable before.

And now these three remain: faith, hope and love. But the greatest of these is love. (1 Cor. 13:13)

Christ, help me to make love my greatest aim in life. Teach me how it's possible to really love everyone because you made them and you love them. Amen.

What's your greatest aim in life?

By God's Wisdom   June 23

The more I learn the more I find yet to learn. Looking at a small flower under a microscope, I realize how intricate and amazing each tiny part of God's creation is. Listening to the many different bird calls makes me think that God cared about giving each bird its own identity. With the entrance of each baby into the world, a new miracle takes place. Hearing scholars answer the same questions with many different answers reminds me that only God knows everything. It makes me wonder how often God looks at the foolishness of our wisdom and wonders why we think we have all the answers.

So you will find favor and good repute in the sight of God and of people. Trust in the LORD with all your heart, and do not rely on your own insight. (Prov. 3:4–5 NRSV)

Your wisdom is vast, O Lord. Grant that I will never think I know more than you've helped me to understand. Amen.

Be content in living with your questions.

Life Is for Living   June 24

The butterflies fluttered wildly in my stomach as the time came closer to give my report in front of the class. It's not a new feeling. I've felt the stress of nervousness many times before.

Stress is often considered bad, something to be avoided. But according to Hans Selye, author of *Stress Without Distress*, stress is a fact of life. "Since stress is associated with all types of activity," he explains, "we could avoid most of it only by never doing anything. Who would enjoy a life of no runs, no hits, no errors?"

God wants me to enjoy living without worrying about the stress that might come. That would merely add more stress.

If God is for us, who can be against us? (Rom. 8:31)

God, help me not to let the threat of stress hinder me from enjoying life, but to trust you to care for me through each trial. Amen.

Let your stressors give you added energy for the day ahead.

Where Is God?   June 25

As I rode through the city, I wondered where God was. All I saw were tall, dark buildings crowded together, with masses of people going in and out of them. Many different noises could be heard: sirens, yelling, screeching brakes. Everyone seemed to be oblivious to those around them.

Then we passed an old building with a beautiful pink flower growing in front of it. It was as if God was calling out, "I'm here too." Then I knew that God had been there all the time. I just hadn't looked hard enough to notice. Wherever I become aware of God, there God is!

They asked each other, "Were not our hearts burning within us while he talked with us on the road and opened the Scriptures to us?" (Luke 24:32)

Thank you, God, for your presence wherever I look for you. Help me as I search for you when you aren't so easy to see. Amen.

Notice God's presence in the eating of a meal today.

—————◆◆—▬▬—◆—————

Open to the Spirit   June 26

The sense of hearing is a funny thing. People can train themselves to not hear certain things. My younger brother became good at not hearing Mother say it was time to do his homework. I can train myself to not hear my alarm clock if I know someone else will hear it and waken me later. The mind can become so accustomed to a sound that the sound no longer makes an impact.

My soul can become so accustomed to the Holy Spirit's call that after a while it, too, is deaf. The longer I block the Spirit from my life, the farther away God's leading will seem. The Holy Spirit is heard only by those who are listening and ready to obey.

Do not put out the Spirit's fire. (1 Thess. 5:19)

Lord, thank you for your gift of the Holy Spirit. I pray that I will always be listening for your guidance in my life. Amen.

Count the number of different sounds you can hear right now.

Follow Me   June 27

I remember the first meeting I attended where an invitation was given for all who wanted to follow Jesus to go forward. I felt Jesus was calling me—my heart pounded wildly, but I was too afraid to go. I wanted more time to think about what all would be involved.

Just recently I was reading in the Gospels about Jesus' calling of the twelve disciples. When Jesus said, "Follow me," the Scriptures say they dropped whatever they were doing and followed him. It doesn't tell us anything about the thoughts and doubts that might have gone through the disciples' heads. Their immediate responses to Jesus' call indicate no hesitancy.

That's how I want my life to be too. When I hear Christ's call, I must answer it without trying to rationalize every move. The twelve disciples are good examples of what it means to live in immediate obedience to Jesus.

As he was walking up the beach he saw Levi, the son of Alphaeus, sitting at his tax collection booth. "Come with me," Jesus told him. "Come be my disciple." And Levi jumped to his feet and went along. (Mark 2:14 LB)

Jesus, let me walk with you, not thinking everything over reasonably, but with the faith that your calling is enough. Amen.

Write a letter from Jesus to you, letting him tell you what he's calling you to do today.

Look for the Open Door June 28

Alexander Graham Bell said, "When one door closes, another opens; but we often look so long and so regretfully upon the closed door that we do not see the one which has opened for us." As an inventor, he probably had to learn to keep looking for new things when other things didn't work.

In much the same way, Christ opens and shuts doors for us. Sometimes shut doors are painful, and it's difficult to see at once the doors that are opening. But if we search diligently, doors will open. God doesn't shut doors unless there's a better one to open.

In him the whole building is joined together and rises to become a holy temple in the Lord. (Eph. 2:21)

Thank you, Jesus, for controlling the doors in my life. Guide me in knowing which are opened and which are closed to me. Amen.

Thank God for a specific open door you've just gone through.

Who Are You Kidding? June 29

When a person refuses to go to church because it's too hot, then goes to the beach instead, who is she kidding? When a person doesn't have enough money to tithe but lives in a nice home, has plenty to eat and wear, and drives a nice car, who is he kidding? When a person can't stay awake during a twenty-minute sermon, yet stays up to watch the late show, who is she kidding? When a person stays away from church because there are too many people, but goes to crowded ball games, who is he kidding? When a person does whatever she wants to do all week, then is too tired to go to church on Sunday, who is she kidding? Not God!

"It is mine to avenge, I will repay," says the Lord. (Rom. 12:19)

O God, grant that I never try to fool you by making silly excuses for not doing what I know is right. Amen.

Sing a song of love to Jesus.

Enriching Compliments   June 30

Everyone has seen what a compliment can do for a person. Mark Twain once said, "I can live for two months on a good compliment." Not only is the recipient of the compliment being blessed, but so is the person giving it. What is said aloud is remembered better and believed longer. Good feelings toward another enrich both sides of the relationship. As Oscar Wilde put it, "It is a great mistake to give up paying compliments, for when we give up saying what is charming, we give up thinking what is charming."

Do not let any unwholesome talk come out of your mouths, but only what is helpful for building others up according to their needs, that it may benefit those who listen. (Eph. 4:29)

Thank you, Lord, for the many times I've been brought happiness by either receiving a compliment or by giving a compliment. Amen.

Think a compliment ... then say it.

MICHAEL SILUK

Believe in God   July 1

At first, "believing" and "believing in" may seem to represent the same idea, but they are really two different concepts. Believing is done in the mind, whereas believing in something calls for action. A step of faith is needed to work for a cause and become completely involved.

Jesus calls his followers not only to believe what he said but also to believe in him. His calling requires both knowledge and the subsequent action to carry out that knowledge successfully.

For God so loved the world that he gave his one and only Son, that whoever believes in him shall . . . have everlasting life. (John 3:16)

I want to be aware of what is involved in believing in you, Jesus. May I never be satisfied to only believe you. Amen

How does your life exemplify that you believe *and* believe in Jesus?

A Sturdy Foundation   July 2

One of my favorite things to do at the beach is to build sand castles. It's fun to see who can build the biggest, sturdiest, and fanciest castle. Each time, however, when I return the next day, the tide has washed them all away. A fishing pier along the same shore has continued to stand through many changes in the tide. Its foundation is deep and sturdy.

No matter how good a job I do building with sand, it's never good enough to last. Neither can I build a good enough protection against the tides of life without Jesus' giving me a deep and sturdy foundation.

But everyone who hears these words of mine and does not put them into practice is like a foolish man who built his house on sand. (Matt. 7:26)

With you, Jesus, I don't need to be washed around like sand on the beach. Thank you for being my Foundation. Amen.

Draw a picture of your life as a building, beginning with its foundation.

Blessings of Rest from Work
July 3

I remember a spring when everything was off to a good start. The fruit trees were full of blossoms, and the gardens were green with early crops. Then came a killing frost, putting an end to the productivity of the orchard and the gardens for that year.

I had a similar experience recently when I was working frantically to do several tasks at once. When I became sick and was forced to stay in bed, I soon found out I wasn't essential for the work after all. Life kept going without me and things got done even when I didn't help.

It doesn't pay to work so hard that I'm completely worn out. Then I'm of no use at all.

O Lord, you have freed me from my bonds and I will serve you forever. (Ps. 116:16 LB)

Thank you, Lord, for showing me when I need to slow down. I give you control of my life to keep working in me. Amen.

Spend one minute in silence, meditating on the word God.

Celebrate! July 4

On the evening of July 4, my brothers, sister, and I went out in the yard to watch the fireworks, which were clearly visible a mile away. They were showy displays, with many beautiful colors spurting out in all directions.

That evening I thought about my Christian life. I wondered if I was making visible the joy and beauty of my life with Christ, not only to those who are close to me but also to those who may be watching from a distance.

If fireworks go all out to celebrate the freedom of our country, how much more reason do I have to celebrate the freedom I experience through Christ!

Let your light shine before others, so that they may see your good works and give glory to your Father in heaven. (Matt. 5:16 NRSV)

Forgive me, Jesus, when I have not shown the joy you give me so that others will know how wonderful you are. Guide me as I seek to spread your love. Amen.

What color do you feel like today?

Christ as the Flashlight July 5

A group of friends and I decided to go camping in the woods one night. Since it was dark when we arrived and there were no lights anywhere around, we used flashlights. As we expected, we easily found our way through the darkness by the light they provided.

Sometimes the world seems dark and scary. I'm not sure what lies ahead. But I can move forward with confidence as Christ lights my path. What looks dark and formidable at first is made much less scary when I know Jesus is with me to light one step at a time.

Your words are a flashlight to light the path ahead of me, and keep me from stumbling. (Ps. 119:105 LB)

Lord, thank you for lighting my path through dark times. Teach me to stay on the path and keep my eyes on you. Amen.

Write about the next step you see being lit for you.

Laugh with Others   July 6

I enjoy telling my younger brother funny stories. He's already laughing so hard when I'm only half done that I hardly need to finish the story. He has a real talent to laugh with others, and this makes him fun to be with.

Everyone needs someone with whom to share joys as well as sorrows. Sometimes being happy with another person is the harder of the two, but it is just as important. If a brother or sister is happy when I'm not, I must learn to forget myself and rejoice with him or her.

Rejoice with those who rejoice. (Rom. 12:15)

Thank you, Lord, for the ability to laugh and share happiness with others. Thank you also for all those who share in my happiness. Amen.

Have a hearty laugh!

Stand Up for Jesus   July 7

"Stand up, stand up for Jesus"—those are words from a hymn written by George Duffield, inspired by a dying minister. The minister had been driven out of his church for speaking out against slavery. When Duffield asked him, on his deathbed, if he had any words for his people he said, "Yes, tell them to stand up for Jesus."

Too many times I fail to stand up for Jesus. I'm content to keep my convictions to myself and not let others know who's in charge of my life. I must remember that if I speak boldly about Jesus, it will encourage others to stand up for him, and Jesus will receive the glory.

Paul and Barnabas spent considerable time there, speaking boldly for the Lord, who confirmed the message of his grace by enabling them to do miraculous signs and wonders. (Acts 14:3)

O Ruler of my life, help me to let others know of you and not to be content to hide your presence within. Amen.

Pray standing.

Admit It   July 8

Some of the most difficult words to say and really mean are "I'm sorry. It's my fault. Will you forgive me?" Yet they're essential to good relationships.

Selfishness tries to rationalize wrong actions and blame another. The longer I wait to confess a wrong, the harder it becomes to do it. The line that says, "Love means never needing to say you're sorry" is all wrong according to Jesus. He loves me more than I can imagine, yet I must confess my sins so Christ can forgive them. Peace can come only through admitting when I'm wrong.

If we confess our sins, he is faithful and just and will forgive us our sins and purify us from all unrighteousness. (1 John 1:9)

Thank you for the reminder, Jesus, that real love says "I'm sorry" many times. Teach me to mirror your unlimited forgiveness. Amen.

Write a prayer of confession.

A New Appearance   July 9

I watched the changes as I rubbed wax on the car, making the once-dull finish so shiny I could see myself in it. I was amazed at the difference cleaning, waxing, and polishing had made.

In a similar way, Christ's redeeming power can make a lot of difference in my life too. By a daily renewal of our relationship the sparkle and appeal of faith can be retained. When I'm willing to submit my life to God for cleaning and polishing, an amazing transformation takes place.

Sprinkle me with the cleansing blood and I shall be clean again. (Ps. 51:7 LB)

Take my life, O God, and clean it with your perfection. Amen.

Wash the dishes and think about God making your life clean.

Work for the Lord   July 10

One summer I worked at a monotonous factory job, stuffing envelopes. The other workers and I had races to see who could stuff the fastest. We listened to the radio, sang, and talked about every imaginable subject to stay awake.

Being of the opinion that everything a Christian does should be for God's glory, I tried to think of what glory God was receiving in what I was doing. I found that even in a monotonous summer job, some good can be found. Working just as hard and fast when the boss isn't watching is one sign of working for a higher authority. Another sign is staying cheerful through the long hours.

Working for God is more rewarding than just receiving a paycheck. The paycheck came only every other week, but God's rewards come after each day of good work.

Work hard and cheerfully at all you do, just as though you were working for the Lord and not merely for your masters, remembering that it is the Lord Christ who is going to pay you. (Col. 3:23–24 LB)

I pray, Lord, that I will always do my best for you at work, even if no one is watching and no matter how hard the job is. Amen.

Do your least favorite job for the glory of God.

God Gives Road Signs   July 11

A friend and I decided to go shopping in a distant town, where neither of us had been before. We started out not knowing the way but confident that with the help of the road signs we wouldn't have any trouble finding our destination.

That kind of experience doesn't sound scary, but it seems when God calls me to leave what I know and travel into the unknown, I'm afraid. I forget that God, too, promises to give me road signs along the way to direct me. When life's road becomes puzzling and intricate, it's comforting to know I'm not on my own for direction.

For this God is our God for ever and ever; he will be our guide even to the end. (Ps. 48:14)

Thank you, my gracious Leader, for guidance down the road you've called me to travel. May I always remember to watch for your road signs. Amen.

Pray, looking at a map as your reminder of your Guide.

------------◆◆━━━◆◆------------

When the Other Person ...   July 12

When the other person acts that way, he's ugly . . .

When you do it, it's nerves.

When she's set in her way, she's obstinate . . .

When you are, it's just firmness.

When he doesn't like your friends, he's prejudiced . . .

When you don't like his, you are simply showing good judgment of human nature.

When she tries to be accommodating, she's polishing the apple . . .

When you do it, you're using tact.

When he takes time to do things, he is dead slow . . .

When you take ages, you are deliberate.

When she picks flaws, she's cranky . . .

When you do, you're discriminating.

These words by an anonymous writer capture the tendency of self-justification that I find in myself when I'm not careful.

For in the same way you judge others, you will be judged, and with the measure you use, it will be measured to you. (Matt. 7:2)

Lord, guide me today and every day to see another's actions as I would my own. Amen.

Say something kind to one with whom you often find fault.

Good Atmosphere   July 13

When human beings first landed on the moon, they discovered many craters on its surface, most of which were caused by meteors. Since the moon has no atmosphere, meteors were not burned up before impact. Scientists estimate that over two hundred million meteors enter the earth's atmosphere each day, but most of them are burned up before they reach the earth.

My heart also must have an atmosphere surrounding it for protection against the threatening meteors of life. It's a defense against the pressures and words thrown at me each day. With Christ in my heart, many situations can be burned down to a size I can handle.

Keep your heart with all vigilance, for from it flow the springs of life. (Prov. 4:23 NRSV)

The atmosphere you give my heart, Lord, will help keep evil from entering. Thank you for your protection. Amen.

Imagine Christ within your heart, radiating an atmosphere of love.

Infections   July 14

Through modern medicine, it's now possible to be inoculated against many kinds of diseases and infections. Other kinds of infections with no medical protection available are also important to guard against. It is impossible to be isolated in life from all disease or all temptation and evil, but much of it can be avoided.

As a Christian, I also have an inoculation against infection in my spiritual life—Jesus. Jesus helps me seek the good things in life, and with both of us working together, I won't be destroyed by the infection of temptation.

How can young people keep their way pure? By guarding it according to your word. (Ps. 119:9 NRSV)

Thank you, Jesus, for being my protection against the infections that threaten my spiritual well-being in this life. Help me overcome the temptations and pressures of my society and live totally for you. Amen.

From what does your spiritual inoculation guard you?

———————

It's Hard to Imagine   July 15

As I stood on the beach watching the waves pound against the shore, I marveled once again at the power of the ocean. People have learned to control many things, but nothing on earth can prevent the tide or stop the waves.

For me the ocean often symbolizes God. It's hard to imagine a God who created the powerful ocean, whose power itself is beyond my perception. It's also hard to imagine why I would ever resist giving my life to the all-powerful God.

I trust in you, O Lord; I say , "You are my God." My times are in your hands. (Ps. 31:14–15)

Thank you, mighty God, for your strength that watches over me all the time. Continue to make your presence known. Amen.

Contemplate the power of God as you imagine the pounding surf of the ocean.

Giving Account   July 16

As a child, when I did something wrong, I tried to blame it on someone else. Sometimes it worked; sometimes it didn't. Today it's still hard for me to take responsibility for my mistakes.

As far back as Cain and Abel, people have provided examples of that human trait of disclaiming responsibility. When God asked Cain where Abel was, Cain responded, "Am I my brother's keeper?"

Occasionally it's possible to pass the responsibility off onto someone else, but we can never fool God. All people are held accountable in the Book of Life for what they do.

And each person was judged according to what he had done. (Rev. 20:13)

Teach me to face up to my own actions, O God. Get rid of that evil in me that I don't want to recognize. Amen.

Look at your life as you think God sees it.

Handling God's Money   July 17

The use of money is a test of character, and a surprising number of verses in the Scriptures speak to the subject. One person claims that in the synoptic gospels, one verse of every six refers to money, either directly or indirectly. Money is involved in sixteen of the Lord's thirty-three parables.

J. Oswald Sanders, in his book A *Spiritual Clinic*, states, "There is often a very definite connection between weakness

in the spiritual life and failure in the stewardship of money."
It is easy to make excuses for not giving to God, but no
excuse is good enough.

**Remembering the words the Lord Jesus himself
said: "It is more blessed to give than to receive."
(Acts 20:35)**

*Your blessings are bountiful, Lord, and everything I have
is from you. Help me to be generous with what you've given
me. Amen.*

**Make a plan for how you will return to God part of
the next money you receive.**

Jesus at Mealtime   July 18

I usually think of a congregation as a large group of
people gathered together in a church building for a specific
service. But Jesus said that if as few as two or three are
congregated in his name, he will be with them.

When the two disciples who were on their way to
Emmaus after Jesus' death walked with Jesus, they didn't
recognize him until he sat down to eat with them.

Jesus is the guest at each meal today, too, when we ask
his blessing on our food. Even though he's not visible as he
was to those disciples, we can be assured of his presence,
which makes mealtimes a worshipful experience.

**When he was at the table with them, he took bread,
gave thanks, broke it and began to give it to them.
(Luke 24:30)**

*Thank you, Jesus, for being my personal companion and
revealing your presence not only when many people are
gathered together in your name. Amen.*

Place an extra chair at the table as you eat to remind you of your invisible Guest.

The Perfect One   July 19

Luke records the story of Jesus telling Simon Peter to let down his net after a night when the fishermen were unable to catch any fish. Peter was astounded by the miraculous results—a huge catch. Realizing Jesus' greatness, Peter recognized the reality of his own sins, and he told Jesus to go away.

It disturbs me, too, when I see my life beside the life of Jesus, the Perfect One. Escape is impossible, and Jesus doesn't want me to leave anyway. He wants me to learn from him. Only by staying beside him through my failures can I learn from his perfection.

When Simon Peter saw this, he fell at Jesus' knees and said, "Go away from me, Lord; I am a sinful man!" (Luke 5:8)

Dear Jesus, thank you for your perfection and your compassion for me, a sinner. Draw me closer to you that I may learn from you. Amen.

Think about Jesus, the Perfect One, loving you.

To the End of the Age   July 20

When I measure myself by Jesus' divine standard, I am quickly put to shame by my shortcomings. But instead of feeling defeated, I could use my sense of shame to improve myself. By having Jesus as my example, I can always ask myself what his will is in any situation. I can improve by seeing myself through his eyes.

Jesus doesn't want me to be so overcome by his greatness that I give up. He promised to be with me to the end of time, to help me to continually become more Christlike. Following him leads to a deep appreciation of the fact that he will never leave me.

And surely I am with you always, to the very end of the age. (Matt. 28:20)

Lord Jesus, help me to look to your example without becoming discouraged. Thank you for your divine guidance. Amen.

Ask Jesus for the grace to look at yourself as he sees you.

God's Word Boomerangs   July 21

My brother received a boomerang as a gift last year. When he threw it into the air, it circled and came back to him. Although he used it as a toy, the real purpose of a boomerang is to kill birds.

God's Word is like a boomerang. It returns only after it has accomplished a purpose. God gives the Word to Christians, trusting them to send it out. I don't need to be afraid when I speak for God. I can be sure God's Word won't return empty when I am an instrument in helping to accomplish its purpose—to glorify God!

So shall my word be that goes forth from my mouth; it shall not return to me empty, but it shall accomplish that which I purpose, and prosper in the thing for which I sent it. (Isa. 55:11 RSV)

Lord God, let me be a boomerang for you in sending forth your Word. Thank you for the words you give me to say. Amen.

What message would you like to boomerang to the world?

———— •• ——•—— •• ————

Going Directly to God   July 22

Shopping in a new grocery store can be frustrating the first few times. Items are hard to find until their location is learned.

I had such an experience when I was asked to get something from a store where I had never been. I looked a long time without success. I didn't ask a clerk because I kept thinking I would soon find it by myself. I finally gave up, however, and asked for help. The clerk showed me exactly where it was.

Life can be like that too. I try to do something on my own until I can't do any more. Then I go crying to God for help. It would be easier if I'd go to God right away instead of persisting in relying only on my own knowledge for so long.

Let us then approach the throne of grace with confidence, so that we may receive mercy and find grace to help us in our time of need. (Heb. 4:16)

Gracious God, forgive me for the times I thought I could handle a situation alone. Thank you for helping me. Amen.

What are you struggling to do alone that God would be glad to help you with?

———— •• ——•—— •• ————

Learning from the Birds

July 23

Within nature there are many lessons waiting to be discovered. I haven't begun to learn all of them, but the birds taught me one.

While bird watching, I listened to the songs of the birds. Each bird sounded different. Then I noticed that they were all singing at once—not just the ones who could sing best, nor the ones with the most beautiful feathers. Each was singing her best, and it didn't seem to bother her a bit if another bird was singing something different.

I have learned from the birds that I need to think less of how my song or anything in my life compares to another person's. I should sing the song God has given me as well as I can and be satisfied with that.

And the birds nest beside the streams and sing among the branches of the trees. (Ps. 104:12 LB)

Great Creator, thank you for the song you've given me to sing. Give me also a joy in singing that refuses to compare my song to another's. Amen.

Listen to the variety of bird songs and let them be a prayer in your consciousness.

Light Out of Darkness

July 24

Our family was with a group of tourists one summer, going through a huge cave beneath the Virginia mountains. The cave was lighted occasionally by electric lights, so we could see the path through what would otherwise have been a dark and dangerous place. When we were far from the entrance, our guide announced that he would turn off the lights so we could feel what darkness really is. It was scary, but I knew the guide had the power to make it light again.

When circumstances in life change suddenly and everything looks dark, it's scary. Fear can be banished, however, by remembering that God has the power to bring light out of darkness. When I put my faith in God, I don't need to walk in the dark.

When darkness overtakes him, light will come bursting in. (Ps. 112:4 LB)

God, O Light of my path, thank you for providing a way out of the darkness that sometimes surrounds me. Amen.

Close your eyes and see the darkness. Then imagine God's light coming closer and closer.

The Greatest Invitation July 25

I read the invitation again. It would be exciting to go to my friend's wedding. Probably a lot of other friends would be there too, and I looked forward to seeing them again.

As I hurried to write my acceptance of the invitation, I remembered another invitation I had accepted many months before. It was from Jesus, who said, "Come to me." I accepted that invitation too, and it has made the biggest difference in my life.

I knew my friend's wedding would be nice. But it couldn't begin to compare to the greatest wedding of all—when Christ comes for the church. At that huge wedding there will be much rejoicing!

The Spirit and the bride say, "Come." And let everyone who hears say, "Come." ... Let anyone who wishes take the water of life as a gift. (Rev. 22:17 NRSV)

Thank you, Father, for your glorious invitation. May I always be worthy of being your guest. Amen.

Write out your acceptance to the "Great Wedding."

━━━━━◆━━◆━━━━◆━━━

The Cost of Worship   July 26

The Bible tells of many times when people traveled far for the sake of Jesus. The Magi traveled for months to see Jesus in the Bethlehem stable. Many people went out to the desert from Jerusalem, Judea, and the Jordan region to hear John the Baptist preach about Jesus' coming. During Jesus' ministry, large crowds followed him everywhere.

How different the story is today! Some have a hard time getting out of bed once a week to go to church. People in Jesus' day would have a hard time understanding why people with so many modern conveniences, easy travel and transportation, and more leisure time than they ever knew, don't have time to go and hear God's Word. Are we taking too much for granted?

Large crowds from Galilee, the Decapolis, Jerusalem, Judea, and the region across the Jordan followed him. (Matt. 4:25)

Forgive me, Lord, for the many times I have taken your Word for granted. Help me to see the foolishness of my excuses to not worship you. Amen.

Imagine Jesus coming to your hometown today. What is your response?

━━━━━◆━━◆━━━━◆━━━

Forgiveness   July 27

"Forgive." I've found that to be one of the most difficult commandments for me to keep. It's not so hard to say I forgive someone, but to let go of the anger and bad memories is often difficult.

Sometimes it doesn't seem fair that I have to forgive people. Then I think of God's forgiveness and never-ending love. It wasn't fair that God's Son, who never sinned, had to die a horrible death on the cross for my sins either—but he did.

By our earthly laws, it doesn't seem right that if I do something wrong, I can have complete forgiveness without paying the consequences, but I can. Even when I knowingly turn my back on God, I'm readily taken back into those loving arms when I want to come. God keeps no records of sins forgiven.

For if you forgive others their trespasses, your heavenly Father will also forgive you; but if you do not forgive others, neither will your Father forgive your trespasses. (Matt. 6:14–15 NRSV)

Lord, teach me complete forgiveness. When I have a difficult time forgiving others, remind me of the many times you've graciously forgiven me and help me to be more Christlike. Amen.

Of what has God forgiven you lately?

Blossom   July 28

The rosebud on the table at the front of the church signified that a baby had been born to one of the families in our congregation. The petals were tightly closed, showing only the beauty of the outer few. Much of the beauty remained inside, hidden until the rose was given time to mature and unfold.

Babies and young Christians are much the same as the rosebud. At first, gifts and talents are undeveloped and can't be seen. But when the bud of faith is nourished by the Holy Spirit, the Word of God, and the family of God, it blossoms out to become a full flower in Christ's work.

They are like trees along a river bank bearing luscious fruit each season without fail. Their leaves shall never wither, and all they do shall prosper. (Ps. 1:3 LB)

Gracious Spirit, bless me with your gifts that I may become beautiful and fruitful for your service. Amen.

What lies yet dormant within your bud?

———— •◆— ◆— •◆ ————

Spiritual Strength   July 29

Sometimes it's hard to get children interested in eating. They don't seem to realize that they need food to give them strength and help them grow. Even if they're hungry, they don't want to take time to eat.

Often Christians act like children. Just as food is needed for physical strength, spiritual strength is found by prayer and reading God's Word. Even when I'm hungry and weak spiritually, I sometimes forget the nourishment I really need. Growth doesn't happen automatically. It takes a lot of time and care. When I am fortified with prayer and God's Word, I have power to let God work through me.

Search for him and for his strength, and keep on searching! (Ps. 105:4 LB)

O Lord, I ask that the desire for spiritual nourishment will become as natural as the desire for food for physical strength. May I always be aware of my need of you. Amen.

How can your desire for spiritual nourishment be increased?

———— •◆— ◆— •◆ ————

King of Kings   July 30

In Handel's oratorio *Messiah* there is a moment that seems to have everyone under its enchantment—when the "Hallelujah Chorus" majestically proclaims, "King of Kings and Lord of Lords . . . forever and ever. Hallelujah!"

No one can yet see everything God is King and Lord over, but we have seen God crowned with honor and glory. We know that nothing can defeat our great God. Jesus rose from the grave and now reigns over all of creation. With God being both the Lord of the universe and my personal Lord, I have nothing to fear from the rulers of this world.

The kingdom of the world has become the kingdom of our Lord and of his Christ, and he will reign for ever and ever. (Rev. 11:15)

Lord God, thank you for ruling my life so I don't need to be concerned about the rulers of this world. Amen.

Who or what rules your life?

Love into Maturity   July 31

My younger brother was delighted when he was given a lively puppy for his birthday. During the weeks that followed, our family learned that having a puppy meant scratches, bites, a messed-up house, ruined clothing, and sometimes a rude awakening in the morning. Through all the irritating things the hyperactive puppy did, however, my brother continued to love and care for him. Because of my brother's patience, the dog eventually calmed down, and everyone enjoyed him.

In the Christian family, some members may require extra patience in their growth. I need to feel the responsibility to

stick by a brother or sister with love, as my own brother loved
his dog into maturity.

**Render true judgments, show kindness and mercy
to one another. (Zech. 7:9 NRSV)**

*Give me patience, Lord, to love people who seem hard to
love at first. Help me to accept them as my brothers and sisters
in your family. Amen.*

**Thank a person who loved you into a growing
maturity.**

Pulling Weeds

When we arrived home from vacation, weeds had taken over our garden. It looked like a hopeless mess. We almost felt that perhaps the best thing to do would be to give it up. Instead, we doubled our efforts to get rid of the weeds so the vegetables could grow freely again.

Life can easily become like a weedy garden. After the seeds of God's goodness are planted, the weeds of temptation come up around the good plants. If the weeds aren't pulled, they will choke out the plants. When I grow discouraged by all the evil I see, I must double my efforts to bring the good into sight again and let it grow freely.

Let us not become weary in doing good, for at the proper time we will reap a harvest if we do not give up. (Gal. 6:9)

Lord, let me not grow weary of keeping the weeds out of my life. Thank you for the strength and courage you give to work at it. Amen.

See yourself in the plants and weeds you see today.

Love Is Sharing

August 2

Recently I received a letter from a close friend in which she was asking herself some questions that made me think too. If I claim that Christ means more to me than anything else, how can I be slow to share him with others? How can I know someone long without telling her what is most important to me? How can I really love a person and yet hold back that which can add unlimited beauty to his life?

The answer is that I can't. To love as Christ loves means sharing his love. Only selfishness can cause me to withhold that most beautiful part of my life—Jesus Christ.

He has given me a new song to sing, of praises to our God. (Ps. 40:3 LB)

Lord Jesus, thank you for the song you've put in my heart to sing for you. Give me courage to sing it out for you in love. Amen.

Rejoice in the memory of a time you shared Christ's love with a friend.

Ruined by Neglect　　　August 3

Wanting to go biking one afternoon, I went to the garage to find the bike I had ridden when I was younger. I was disappointed to see rust and dust covering the frame, flat tires, and crooked handlebars.

Neglect can ruin my life with Christ too. If I don't continue to use what I know and mature in my faith, I will become as useless as the bicycle that was stored away without being ridden or cared for. I can keep growing, however, by continuing to use and practice what I already know.

But those who do what is true come to the light, so that it may be clearly seen that their deeds have been done in God. (John 3:21 NRSV)

Forgive me, Jesus, for times when I've neglected putting your Word into practice. Thank you for your reminder to keep growing. Amen.

Flex some unused muscles.

Celebrate Christmas in August
August 4

Summer is the easiest time of the year for me to become self-centered, but there's really no excuse for it. Being out of school provides more time to give to others.

Christmas is perhaps the busiest time of the year, but people usually find time in the Christmas season to sing at nursing homes, visit friends, give gifts, and do many other special things. And at that point, I resolve to find time to practice the Christmas spirit throughout the entire year. It may even be more rewarding to be kind to people when they aren't expecting it!

And God is able to make all grace abound to you, so that in all things at all times, having all that you need, you will abound in every good work. (2 Cor. 9:8)

Lord, give me the Christmas spirit in August and in every other month of the year. Show me ways to portray your love all year long. Amen.

Give a Christmas gift.

A New Creation
August 5

My grandfather is good at fixing things. Anything from a broken toy to an old piece of furniture looks like new after it has visited his workshop. We have many things in our home proving his skill.

God is the most skilled crafter of all, changing lives. Through Christ, God reconciles us so that we are new creatures. God is patient, working day after day to produce the best possible results in my life. I am the proof of God's skill, the representation of God's love and care.

Therefore, if anyone is in Christ, he is a new creation. (2 Cor. 5:17)

Thank you, Father, for making me into a new creature. I pray that others will know you by seeing the difference you've made in my life. Amen.

Look in the mirror at a new creation.

———————•◆•——◆—————•◆•———————

Love Is Not Blind   August 6

Of love, Rabbi Julius Gordon wrote these words:

Love is not blind—it sees more, not less.
But because it sees more, it is willing to see less.

This kind of love has its supreme example in God. God knows my faults better than anyone, yet he loves me more than anyone else ever can. I too am called to this kind of love. If I find it hard to love someone, maybe I haven't seen enough to be willing to see less.

Forgive as the Lord forgave you. And over all these virtues put on love, which binds them all together in perfect unity. (Col. 3:13–14)

God, thank you for your amazing love. Show me how to look at others through your eyes so that I may grow in love and in the ability to see fewer faults in others. Amen.

Walk in another's shoes.

———————•◆•——◆—————•◆•———————

A Traffic Jam   August 7

It was a hot day, and our family was in the midst of a long line of cars that seemed to be standing still. The heat and slow pace of traffic made traveling miserable, and complaining didn't help either! So we made up games to play. Progress was slow, but eventually we were on our way.

By the following week, the important thing wasn't the time it had taken to get home that afternoon, but how we had spent that time together. Sometimes I want to go at a different pace from the one God wants me to go. I need to remember that how I live is more important than how fast I go.

But do not forget this one thing, dear friends: With the Lord a day is like a thousand years, and a thousand years are like a day. (2 Peter 3:8)

Lord, too often I want to go at a different speed from the one that life demands. Thank you for being the traffic director for me to follow. Amen.

Travel somewhere by foot at a leisurely pace.

Strength in Gentleness   August 8

The harshest, cruelest street gangs make it to the "top." Leaders are considered greatest who act the toughest. Actually, however, these people are not the strong individuals. It is the weak and insecure who feel a need to defend themselves. They try to prove to themselves and to others that they can handle anything.

Only the strong can be gentle. They do not need to prove their strength or defend themselves. Jesus is the best example of this. He's the greatest and also the most gentle.

Christ's Spirit provides the qualities of kindness, generosity, friendliness, and gentleness.

Your gentleness has made me great. (2 Sam. 22:36 LB)

Gentle Savior, grant that I will seek gentleness to prove my strength. Guide me in your steps of greatness. Amen.

Be gentle with a child.

———————

Growing Love   August 9

A friend of mine often tells me things about his father, whom he admires greatly. Even though I haven't ever met this man personally, I think of him as a great person too.

Love for Jesus grows in the same way. Reading accounts in the Bible by those closest to him and hearing other Christians talk about his love helps my love for him to grow. This is how I can learn to know God best until that wonderful day when we will meet face to face.

I pray that out of his glorious riches he may strengthen you with power through his Spirit in your inner being, so that Christ may dwell in your hearts through faith. (Eph. 3:16–17)

God of heaven and earth, thank you for your bountiful love shown to me through your Word and your servants. May I, too, show others your love. Amen.

Read a story about Jesus in one of the gospels.

———————

The Bond in Jesus   August 10

While on a vacation, a group of friends and I stopped at a little country church on Sunday morning. We felt at home immediately as the preacher introduced us to the rest of the congregation. After the service many came to talk to us individually, and we were invited several places for lunch.

Miles from home, we had found fellowship with others who were gathered for the same purpose—to worship God. They were our brothers and sisters even though we had never met before, and it is Jesus who makes this real. We are united by the common bond of Jesus' love into fellowship with each other, no matter where or who we are.

And God placed all things under his feet and appointed him to be head over everything for the church, which is his body. (Eph. 1:22–23)

Thank you, Lord Jesus, for the bond that unifies all of your children through your love. We are truly blessed. Amen.

Pray for all your Christian family as you look at a globe.

Detours of Life   August 11

Traveling down an interstate highway, we were suddenly forced to turn off the road by a detour sign. We didn't know the way on the new road, but we followed the signs.

The back road was much more scenic than the highway. Even though we felt lost at first, we enjoyed the ride through the countryside. Eventually the signs led us back to the familiar road.

Occasionally, God puts detour signs in my path to add extra spots of interest. At first I don't always appreciate being thrown off my course, and I feel lost; but when I follow the rest of the signs and come safely to the end, I can often see the purpose of the detour.

God is my strong refuge, and has made my way safe. (2 Sam. 22:33 RSV)

Thank you, Father, for the detours you place in my life
that turn out so beautifully even when I'm skeptical at first.
Teach me to follow your signs. Amen.

Look for meaning in your interruptions.

Give   August 12

Robert J. McCraken, in one of his sermons, said:

> *Love ever gives,*
> *Forgives, outlives,*
> *And ever stands*
> *With open hands.*
> *And while it lives,*
> *It gives.*
> *For this is love's prerogative—*
> *To give, and give, and give.*

The giving spirit of love becomes evident as I look at
those who love me. Those who truly love don't think of what
they will receive. They think only of how they can give more
and more. This is the kind of love God desires for me.

But just as you excel in everything—in faith, in
speech, in knowledge, in complete earnestness and
in your love for us—see that you also excel in this
grace of giving. (2 Cor. 8:7)

Lord, be with me as I seek to love others. Teach me to give
without expecting anything in return. Amen.

Give an anonymous gift.

The Plank in My Eye   August 13

It was a beautiful day. Many of our neighbors were taking advantage of the nice weather and had hung their wash outside to dry. Suddenly, with little warning, a cloudburst sent them all dashing out to rescue what was already wet. I smiled to myself, glad that we had washed our clothes the day before.

When the rain was over, I remembered something that put an end to my smugness. I had slept outdoors the night before, and in the morning I'd hung my sleeping bag over the clothesline to air out. It was soaked. That taught me a good lesson—to take a good look at myself before I laugh at others.

Why do you see the speck in your neighbor's eye, but do not notice the log in your own eye? (Matt. 7:3 NRSV)

God, thank you for humorous ways of teaching me lessons. May I remember this lesson when I'm tempted to laugh at the misfortunes of others. Amen.

Take an attitude inventory.

Fruit Bearing   August 14

A small cherry tree stands in the yard beside our house. When my brothers, sister, and I were small, we spent many hours in it, climbing its branches, swinging from the lowest boughs, and pretending to drive it as a car. Through all the abuse we gave the tree, it has continued to bear fruit each year.

The cherry tree has a powerful lesson to teach. The ingratitude of others is not an adequate reason for me to stop bearing fruit. Jesus provides the encouragement to continue growing in the Spirit's fruit, even without appreciation.

This is to my Father's glory, that you bear much fruit, showing yourselves to be my disciples. (John 15:8)

Thank you, Lord, for the strength to continue bearing fruit through the hardships others may give. Grant that I will be an encouragement to others to bear good fruit. Amen.

What fruit do you feel most like?

———◆———◆———

Don't Destroy—Enjoy!   August 15

Alongside nearly every road I travel, I see paper, tin cans, and other litter. Few rivers or streams are without debris that people have discarded. Even the sky is filled with pollution.

Sometimes I wonder how God must feel about the way we are ruining this beautiful world. I do know one thing, however. Each person who cares enough to take part in cleaning up or in preventing further destruction makes God happy. I need to remember that the earth is God's gift to enjoy—not destroy.

The earth belongs to God! Everything in all the world is his! (Ps. 24:1 LB)

Thank you, O Wonderful Creator, for this beautiful world to live in. Guide me in ways of conservation rather than destruction. Amen.

Run the faucet less.

———◆———◆———

In God's Light   August 16

Mornings are the most embarrassing times for someone who hasn't washed the windows recently. The bright sunlight shows clearly every dirty spot previously hidden by the darkness of the night.

That's how my life is. If I live in the darkness of sin, my ways don't appear to be bad. In fact, compared to others, they may seem good. But when I live in God's light, the flaws are easily seen. To perfect my life, I need to continue seeing it surrounded by God's righteousness.

I have come into the world as a light, so that no one who believes in me should stay in darkness. (John 12:46)

Thank you for shining in my life, O God, to show me what needs to be polished. Amen.

Look through your God-lit window on the events and thoughts of yesterday.

Pearls from Sand   August 17

The activities of an oyster beautifully illustrate the reactions Christians should have to trouble. The oyster begins to work when a tiny piece of sand enters its shell. With great care, patience, and time, it builds layer after layer of a milky substance around the sand, covering each sharp corner. Eventually a pearl is formed around what was a problem to the oyster.

My natural instinct isn't to make each problem into something beautiful, but it's possible with God's grace.

And the Lord replied, "I myself will go with you and give you success." (Exod. 33:14 LB)

Be with me, Lord, as the sands of life come near me, that I may transform them into pearls of beauty.

What grain of sand is irritating you?

Thank You   August 18

A few months ago I received a thank-you letter from the mother of one of my friends. It brightened my day, and even though I hadn't known her well before, I felt close to her because of her kind words. The time she took to write the letter meant a lot to me.

It made me think of how often I have many reasons to show my appreciation to friends and to God, but neglect doing anything. Appreciation, when given, strengthens the relationship. When I feel far away from God, I could be drawn closer by thinking of things I'm thankful for and telling God about them.

It is good to say, "Thank you" to the Lord, to sing praises to the God who is above all gods. (Ps. 92:1 LB)

Gracious God, teach me the full meaning of thanksgiving. May I learn to show my praise and gratitude more often. Thank you for giving me so much to be thankful for. Amen.

Write a thank-you note to God.

Working Together
for Good   August 19

Some time ago I decided to spend a short vacation with one of my friends. I considered various ways to get there, but nothing was working out. I felt that God was shutting the doors to me, so I decided not to go.

Then during that time I was given a rare opportunity to go somewhere else, where I was greatly enriched. A couple months later God provided me with another chance to visit my friend. Both experiences, as well as seeing God work in a beautiful way, added so much to my life.

Paul knew what he was talking about when he said that "all things work together for good to them that love God."

Yet not as I will, but as you will. (Matt. 26:39)

Thank you, God for directing me in the ways you know to be best. Why would I ever want to neglect your will? Amen.

Watch for God's surprises.

No Instant Replay   August 20

One of the miracles of the modern video camera is instant replay. Only seconds after an exciting event has taken place, it can be seen again.

Life cannot be replayed like that. A bad day can never be taken back, and a good day can never be redone. I cannot live on yesterdays. Each day must be new with fresh vitality. I can retain the beauty of each day only when I see it as a new gift from God.

I will praise you, my God and King, and bless your name each day and forever. (Ps. 145:1 LB)

Thank you, my God, for this beautiful day to praise you. May I see each day as a new gift from you to use for your glory. Amen.

Cherish the present moment.

Be Ready   August 21

I once read of a man who said that he was waiting till his last moment to give his life to Christ. He wanted to live his own life on earth, but he wanted to spend eternity with Jesus in heaven.

His way of living, however, seems like wasted time. Besides missing the blessings and joy of living with Christ now, he may never know the joy of living with him at all. We aren't always able to recognize our last moments. Jesus said that we are to be ready at all times.

So you also must be ready, because the Son of Man will come at an hour when you do not expect him. (Matt. 24:44)

Dear Lord, I thank you that it's not important for me to know when my last moments will be. Help me to be ready all the time. Amen.

Live today as if it were your last.

A Promise-Keeper   August 22

Early in childhood, I realized that whatever my parents told me was the truth. They never lied to me, and they kept their promises.

That helped me to trust in God as I grew older. God has made many promises in the Bible. By seeing humans keep their promises, I have faith that God, through Christ, will also keep his promises.

For no matter how many promises God has made, they are "Yes" in Christ. (2 Cor. 1:20)

O God, teach me to know your ways and rely on your promises. Thank you for human examples of your trustworthiness. Amen.

Tell the truth.

———————

On the Rock   August 23

A friend and I sat on a large rock, watching the river swirl swiftly past. We felt secure in the fact that as long as we stayed on that firm rock, we were safe. Many other rocks surrounded our perch, but they seemed more unstable, slippery, and dangerous; so we stayed where we were.

Watching the water flow past gave me a sense of peace, as if nothing else mattered. Staying on the rock kept me from being pulled downstream with the current.

In life, with Christ as the Rock, the same thing is true. I can be at peace, knowing that even though everything around me is unsteady, when I depend on Jesus to hold me up, I don't have to be afraid of being swept along by other attitudes, temptations, or desires.

Yes, he alone is my Rock, my rescuer, defense and fortress. Why then should I be tense with fear when troubles come? (Ps. 62:2 LB)

You are my Rock, Lord, on whom I can depend when life seems to swirl too fast around me. Thank you. Amen.

Imagine the peace of sitting on a huge, stable rock in a swiftly moving river.

———————

Jesus Wept   August 24

In our culture crying is sometimes considered a sign of weakness. No one, particularly males, should ever be caught crying.

Jesus, on the other hand, who was the strongest and most gentle person who ever lived, wasn't afraid to cry. His tears showed the love he had for Lazarus, his friend who had died. His tears were a sign of great love—not weakness. Instead of trying to hold my tears in, I can thank God for providing a release for my hurts and compassion for others.

Jesus wept. Then the Jews said, "See how he loved him!" (John 11:35–36)

Thank you, Jesus, for your example and for my freedom to shed tears without shame. Amen.

When was the last time you cried?

Reaching the Goal   August 25

I like the story of a girl who had three suitors. She suggested they run a race, and the one who caught her would be her husband.

She filled her pockets with money, and they all began to run. As the first suitor came close to her, she dropped some money in his path. As he stopped to pick it up, she escaped. The same thing happened to her second pursuer.

The money did not dissuade the third young man, however. He continued running and caught the girl for his wife. He treasured her above the money.

Like the last suitor, I must not be sidetracked by anything that may be put in my path and keep me from reaching Christ. Only by continuing the race will I win the prize.

I press on toward the goal to win the prize for which God has called me heavenward in Christ Jesus. (Phil. 3:14)

Guide me in the race to you, Lord, that I may always keep you as my goal.

List the things that have fallen in your path as you race to God.

———————◆—◆◆—◆———————

Thank You, God   August 26

My sister has a devotional book that has space after each day's meditation for writing a prayer. Being given permission to read what she had written, I noticed that most of her sentences began with "Thank you . . ." Knowing of some rough times she had had, I turned to those days. To my surprise, I found only praise in the midst of those troubles as well! I have remembered those prayers since the day I read them, and they have been a continual inspiration to me. I, too, can find something to praise God for in every situation, if I'm willing to try.

I will praise you, my God and King, and bless your name each day and forever. (Ps. 145:1 LB)

Thank you, my God, for my sister and the influence her attitude has had on me. Thank you for giving me something to praise you for every day of my life. Amen.

Praise God for who he is.

———————◆—◆◆—◆———————

Christ's Hands   August 27

It was a great day when I was first asked to baby-sit for several children. I felt honored that the parents trusted me enough to go away, having confidence that I would take good care of their children.

It was a much greater day of responsibility when Jesus returned to heaven. Before he left, he put the work of witnessing to God's love into the hands of his followers. They were to continue it for him, to function as his hands, feet, ears, and heart on earth.

Christ still calls me, as a disciple, to that work. It's a great privilege to be trusted to care for the unsaved of the world.

Therefore go and make disciples of all nations. (Matt. 28:19)

Lord, let me be a tool for your ministry. Thank you for giving me the great responsibility of being a worker for you. Amen.

Draw God's heart; draw your heart.

Encouragement on the Hills   *August 28*

Climbing a steep hill, I was pleased to meet a friend who stopped for a while to talk. Not only was the conversation good, but it also gave me a chance to rest before continuing the hard climb.

The road of life is sometimes steep too. It is a beautiful thing to have friends who encourage me by stopping to talk. It is also beautiful when I can provide a rest stop and brighten someone else's climb.

Two are better than one, because they have a good reward for their toil. For if they fall, one will lift up the other. (Eccl. 4:9–10 NRSV)

Direct me, O great Encourager, in paths that cross with others', so we may refresh each other. Amen.

Encourage one who is tired.

―――――――― ·· ―‑·‑― ·· ――――――――

Jesus Is the Way   August 29

Bees are interesting creatures. When one bee finds a field of flowers, it returns to the hive and flies in a certain pattern. From this pattern the other bees know in which direction the field is and exactly how far to fly to get there.

God sent Jesus into the world to tell us what the greatest gift on earth is and how to receive it. The only way to know God is through his Son. When I look to Jesus, I am guided to the treasure of life, both now and hereafter.

Jesus answered, "I am the way and the truth and the life. No one comes to the Father except through me." (John 14:6)

Thank you, God, for sending Jesus to show me the way to you. Bless my struggle to follow his lead. Amen.

Imagine listening to Jesus as he tells you what God is like.

―――――――― ·· ―‑·‑― ·· ――――――――

Fruitful in Christ   August 30

When my family and I returned from a vacation, I ran to check my row of cantaloupe in the garden. I had spent many hours watering and weeding plants, and the fruit should have been almost ripe by now. When I got to the garden, however, I was disappointed to find that in my absence our duck had waddled down the middle of the row, breaking and killing many of the vines.

Christ must suffer many times when, after he nurtures a person's growth, something destroys the vines of communication and fellowship between him and the believer. Without being connected to Christ I can't continue to produce the Spirit's fruit.

Remain in me, and I will remain in you. No branch can bear fruit by itself; it must remain in the vine. (John 15:4)

Grant, O Lord, that nothing will sever the vines of communication connecting us, so that I will bear much fruit. Thank you for being the Vine. Amen.

Imagine yourself as a plant being nourished by Christ.

———————

Gifts   August 31

The following words by Francis Maitland Balfour have a lot of meaning for me. When I practice what they say, my life is filled with joy.

The best thing to give to your enemy is forgiveness; to an opponent, tolerance; to a friend, your heart; to your child, a good example; to your father, deference; to your mother, conduct that will make her proud of you; to yourself, respect; to all people, charity.

And now these three remain: faith, hope and love. But the greatest of these is love. (1 Cor. 13:13)

Dear God, help me to know what it is to love all people, to forgive my enemy, and to be a good example to others as you have done. Amen.

Who is looking to you as an example?

———————

CLEO FREELANCE PHOTO

Christt, My Pilot September 1

I remember seeing a reproduction of Warner Sallman's painting *Christ, Our Pilot*. In the painting, a young man is steering his boat through stormy waters. The sky is dark with clouds, pierced by streaks of lightning. Jesus is portrayed standing behind the youth, with one hand on his shoulder and the other pointing forward. Jesus is not taking over the helm, but simply showing the way and remaining by his side to give comfort.

At my invitation, Christ becomes the Pilot of my life. I'm not forced to go a certain way but am patiently led in the best route. I choose to follow Jesus' way in faith.

The apostles said to the Lord, "Increase our faith!" (Luke 17:5)

Thank you, God, for being my Guide and Protector in the course of life. I pray that I will never be satisfied to be my own pilot. Amen.

Pray, putting yourself in the picture, and imagine Jesus' one hand on your shoulder and his other pointing the direction.

Created in God's Image September 2

I pursue God. I am pursued by God. I listen to God. God listens to me. I talk to God. God talks to me. I am created by God, and I am co-creator with God in shaping my life.

Part of being created in the image of God is that I am created with what Augustine called a God-shaped vacuum— a need to be in relationship with God. And to make that more tangible, I am given a way of seeing and knowing God more easily—Jesus. Of all the cults and religions that strive to reach the Supreme Being, the best one I've found is the revelation of God in Jesus Christ.

Create in me a pure heart, O God, and renew a steadfast spirit within me. (Ps. 51:10)

Thank you, God, for creating me in your image. Thank you, too, for making your revelation known to me through Jesus. Amen.

How are you filling your emptiness—your need for God?

God's Everlasting Love   September 3

Even though some of my trials seem to last a long time, each has an end. God's love continues throughout and helps me through them all. I like the poem by P. Gerhardt that says:

> *All my life I still have found,*
> *And I will forget it never,*
> *Every sorrow hath its bound,*
> *And no cross endures forever.*
> *All things else have but their day,*
> *God's love only lasts for aye.*

He will not break the bruised reed, nor quench the dimly burning flame. He will encourage the faint-hearted, those tempted to despair. (Isa. 42:3 LB)

Thank you, God, for your love that covers every trial and sorrow I have. Amen.

Check the brightness of your burning flame.

Aglow with God's Presence
September 4

As I watched and listened to the preacher before me, I suddenly realized why he had become a favorite of mine. Not only did he speak of joy in Christ, but the radiance on his face also spoke of that joy. I knew by looking at him that Christ's Spirit filled his heart.

After the service, I told him of my appreciation for his happy face. To my surprise, he hadn't realized that he was smiling during the sermon. It was another example to me of how Christ can work even subconsciously when I give up my own control.

Moses didn't realize as he came back down the mountain with the tablets that his face glowed from being in the presence of God. (Exod. 34:29 LB)

Lord, I pray that I too will glow with the Spirit of your presence. Thank you for being so real. Amen.

What expression will others encounter in you today?

———————— •◆• —◆— •• ————————

Freedom of Choice
September 5

How well I remember the free feeling of being away from home for the first time. I was enjoying a week of summer camp, free to do anything without worrying about what my parents would say. When exercising my new freedom, however, I found that I could be happy only by doing what I knew my parents would want.

Jesus also gives me freedom to choose what I will do. I've found, however, that I can be truly happy only when I'm within Christ's will.

As servants of God, live as free people, yet do not use your freedom as a pretext for evil. (1 Peter 2:16 NRSV)

Thank you, Jesus, for the freedom of choice you have given me. Guide me in using my freedom for your glory. Amen.

Recognize your freedom in Christ.

It Takes Time   September 6

Not much of Jesus' life between the ages of twelve and thirty is revealed. He probably spent a lot of time with his parents, learning to live as a human, and with his heavenly Father, learning how to minister as the divine Son of God.

The disciples also spent time in training. They followed, observed, and questioned Jesus for three years before they were sent out on their own to minister. I'm often too anxious to know and do everything right away. I, too, need to be patient with myself in learning the ways of Jesus.

And he said to them, "Follow me, and I will make you fish for people." (Matt. 4:19 NRSV)

Give me patience, Jesus, to follow you, learning things as you teach me. Thank you for your example. Amen

Write in your journal about how it feels to be your age.

Tune Up   September 7

I watched as a musician tuned his guitar. Pitches that sounded all right to me didn't satisfy him, so he worked until every string was perfectly in tune. Since he was a better musician than I, he was better able to tell when the strings needed to be tightened or loosened.

When I'm tempted to think my life is faultless, maybe I'm not sensitive enough to what is good and what is bad. Just as the musician develops a good ear to tune instruments, I can develop, over time, a good conscience to tune my life to Christ.

Do not be overcome by evil, but overcome evil with good. (Rom. 12:21)

Teach me, Lord, to know when my life is out of tune with your will. Help me to develop a good conscience to guide me. Amen.

Is there a "string" in your life that needs to be tightened? ... loosened?

God Works Through the Ordinary
September 8

Sometimes when I'm working at home, I wish I could be doing more than the regular chores of a household. Then I'm reminded of Rebekah's story, found in Genesis; it helps me to be satisfied with whatever I'm doing.

As Rebekah was performing her usual chore of drawing water from the well, Abraham's servant asked her for a drink. Her willingness and kindness changed the rest of her life. What I'm doing isn't always as important as what kind of an attitude I have. God works through ordinary events too.

Then she said, "I'll draw water for your camels, too, until they have enough!" (Gen. 24:19 LB)

Thank you, God, that I can be assured of your guidance in all the activities of my life. Amen.

Give yourself a treat!

———————

Control of New Experiences
September 9

I watched as my brother trained his horse for riding. To get the horse accustomed to weight, my brother put bags of sand on her back. Many days later he saddled her. After more waiting and training, my brother was finally able to mount.

When Jesus rode into Jerusalem, he sat on an unbroken colt. That in itself was a miracle. He had complete control of the colt when the crowd was yelling, throwing clothes down for it to walk on, and waving palm branches. If Jesus was able to keep that unbroken colt calm, I can trust him to keep me calm and guide me in new experiences.

Go to the village ahead of you, and just as you enter it, you will find a colt tied there, which no one has ever ridden. (Mark 11:2)

Lord, I want the same strong hands that calmed the colt on the way to Jerusalem to be my guide on the way to my heavenly home. Amen.

Be still and soak in Jesus' calmness.

———————

Learning to Love
September 10

As the teacher read the new seating chart, I found myself sitting beside a girl I hardly knew. I had never talked to her, and I knew she wouldn't be easy to love. Her impatience caused her to have few friends.

As I learned more about her throughout the year and became her friend, I understood how her physical ill health and an abusive family situation made patience especially hard. I wondered if I could have been even as patient as she was in her situation.

Christ didn't tell me to love only those whom I understand. Sometimes I must first show kindness to the unlovely, and then I will be shown why they were hard to love.

Therefore be imitators of God, as beloved children, and live in love, as Christ loved us. (Eph. 5:1–2 NRSV)

When I don't understand someone, Jesus, give me patience to love that person anyway. Maybe a friend is just what he or she needs. Thank you for your example. Amen.

Be interested in another.

————◆─◆◆─◆◆————

Icebergs and People   September 11

Like the person I mentioned yesterday, other people I didn't appreciate at first have become my friends. I have learned that people are like icebergs. The little bit that is seen doesn't nearly begin to portray all that lies beneath the surface.

Shy people are like that. At first there doesn't seem to be much to them because they aren't easy to get to know. But when I'm willing to spend time with them and dig deeper for meaning, all people become unique and beautiful in their own way. If people seem uninteresting, it's probably because I don't know them well enough yet.

Accept one another, then, just as Christ accepted you, in order to bring praise to God. (Rom. 15:7)

Give me patience, Lord, to learn to know people before I judge their worth. Teach me to look deep enough to see their beauty. Amen.

Explore beneath the tip of an "iceberg."

Strong Builders for Christ
September 12

Two of my uncles are housing contractors, and they know the importance of precise work. If they build carelessly, even though others may not notice at first, after several years things will begin to fall apart. Their good reputations and jobs will be lost.

Life can be compared to building a house. Every thought, act, and decision I make is being added to the construction of my life and determines in what kind of a building I live. Even if I try to hide the bad parts, they will sooner or later be my downfall. Each choice I make helps to determine how strong my house is becoming.

For God will bring every deed into judgment, including every hidden thing, whether it is good or evil. (Eccl. 12:14)

Thank you, God, for the reminder that each step I take in building my life is important. Guide me in each decision. Amen.

Make a choice for strength.

Before I Ask
September 13

When I meet new friends who become especially close to me, I sometimes think about the fact that God gave them to me before I asked for anyone. God knows my needs and provides for them before I realize the needs myself. It's a good feeling to know that in a world where we are all expected to take care of ourselves, I have a Protector who takes care of me better than I ever could myself.

And I will also give you what you didn't ask for—riches and honor! (1 Kings 3:13 LB)

Thank you, Lord, for meeting needs in my life that I may not even be aware of. You are truly a great and wonderful God. Amen.

List the needs that have been met in your life in the past week.

Love Notes   *September* 14

The first months in a new school, with new classmates and teachers, can be lonely at times. That was my experience when I transferred to a different high school. An event that has stayed in my memory is the note that a classmate gave me one day. What she said wasn't especially important, but just knowing that she cared enough to spend time to let me know it was a tremendous lift!

She and other friends have continued writing these short "love notes," and each time it makes my whole day better! I've found that an even greater blessing is to give to others. A note of sincere appreciation is well worth the little bit of time it takes to write it.

Therefore, encourage one another and build each other up. (1 Thess. 5:11)

Lord, thank you for friends. Show me someone today whose life I could brighten by a love note of encouragement and appreciation. Amen.

Write and give a love note.

Building Character   September 15

When pure gold and pure silver are pressed together, even for a short time, part of each is buried in the other. Unless they're put under a microscope, however, that fact is often unnoticeable.

People are like that too. Part of me is imbedded in each person I touch with my presence, and I receive bits from each person too. It may not be immediately evident, but it's still true.

I can choose what kind of bits I want to plant in others by guarding my thoughts and limiting my actions to what will help to strengthen them. I'm also responsible for what I allow to be rubbed off of them on to me.

Let us therefore make every effort to do what leads to peace and to mutual edification. (Rom. 14:19)

Lord, guide my ways so that I will always seek to edify those with whom I come in contact. Amen.

What kind of "fleck" will you leave imbedded in another today?

———•———•———•———

Rest   September 16

Rest is not quitting
    The busy career;
Rest is the fitting
    Of self to its sphere.
'Tis loving and serving
    The highest and best!
'Tis onward, unswerving—
    And that is true rest.

—J. S. Dwight

I used to think of rest as laziness or inaction; but, as Dwight has helped me to understand, rest is inner peace and quiet. One who rests in such a way feels and acts in God's will. Rest is more than a break from work. It is a whole dimension of life.

Now we who have believed enter that rest. (Heb. 4:3)

I give myself to you, God, to do your will. Then I may also rest in your peace. Amen.

Rest in God.

Keep Exercising   *September 17*

I once heard of an elderly man who jogged a mile every morning to maintain his good health. He had exercised in this way every day for years, and he knew that if he was to stay in shape now, he couldn't stop.

I need to exercise the fruit of the Holy Spirit in my life each day as well, to stay in spiritual shape. I can never be content to have reached a certain maturity in my Christian life and then stop exercising. I can stay healthy in Christ only by exercising the Word in my life each day.

Therefore, since we are surrounded by such a great cloud of witnesses, let us throw off everything that hinders and the sin that so easily entangles, and let us run with perseverance the race marked out for us. (Heb. 12:1)

Keep me mindful, Lord, of the daily exercise I need if I am to stay in shape with you. Thank you for giving me strength to stay healthy in you. Amen.

Memorize Hebrews 12:1.

Making Friends Can Be Hard

September 18

When I was younger, Dad had a job in which he traveled a lot. On some of his shorter trips, our family accompanied him, and this meant meeting many new people. Until I learned to know someone in the new surroundings, I felt awkward. By the time we left it was often difficult, however, to say good-bye to a new friend. Meeting people can be frightening, but by keeping a few things in mind, it can be fun:

1. The other person is probably just as shy as I am, so someone might as well make the first move—why not me?
2. We probably have at least one thing in common—I should take time to find out what it is.
3. The sooner I get to know that person, the longer I'll have to enjoy the new-found friendship.

I don't want to miss out on a fun relationship just because I'm too shy to say "hi."

Love your neighbor as yourself. (Rom. 13:9)

Thank you, Lord, for so many beautiful people. Thank you, too, for opportunities to learn to know more of your sons and daughters who help me feel closer to you. Amen.

Imagine that a stranger wishes you would say "hi."

To Find the Lost

September 19

I remember well the day we lost our new dog. The whole family and many neighbors became concerned. We spent hours searching the woods and driving around looking for him. Many phone calls were made to ask people to be on the lookout for him. Finally, in the evening, he was found. Our friends and neighbors rejoiced with us over his return.

How much greater is the rejoicing over one person who leaves the sinful life behind and makes an appearance in God's kingdom!

Then he calls his friends and neighbors together and says, "Rejoice with me; I have found my lost sheep." (Luke 15:6)

O Lord, give me concern for those who haven't found their home in you. Show me ways I can help them find you. Amen.

Pray for a friend who doesn't know Christ.

The Greatest Inheritance — September 20

When my grandparents moved to a smaller house, they gathered their children together to give them many of their possessions. They gave away dishes, furniture, and books they had collected over the years—things that would now find use in their children's families.

God has been preparing a kingdom for the faithful in Christ ever since the world was created. God looks forward to the day when all these will be called together and given their place in his eternal home. My hope is in the day I will be able to claim my share in this tremendous inheritance.

Come, you who are blessed by my Father; take your inheritance, the kingdom prepared for you since the creation of the world. (Matt. 25:34)

Thank you, Lord, for the inheritance of your kingdom, in which I have the privilege of sharing. Amen.

Image the inheritance Christ has for you.

God Knows All   September 21

At a party I was taken out of the room where my friends were and was told that we were playing a game. When I went back, I was led to the center of the circle. Not a word was said, but everyone stared at me. They seemed to look right through me. I soon became so uncomfortable that I left the room again. Then they explained that they merely wanted to see my reactions to the staring and silence.

God is always watching me and really does see right through me to all I do, say, and think. I must be careful to do only what I know is pleasing and acceptable in God's sight.

There is nothing concealed that will not be disclosed, or hidden that will not be made known. (Luke 12:2)

O God, guide me in the ways you want me to go, so I don't need to be afraid to let my words or actions be heard or seen. Thank you for the strength I know you can give. Amen.

How does it feel to realize that God knows everything about you?

Responsibility in Love   September 22

The trailer my cousin was sleeping in caught on fire one night. Being a heavy sleeper, she didn't wake up at first, but her dog jumped on her again and again until she realized what was happening. He may have saved her life.

Many people are sleeping today, unaware of how little time they have to wake up and leave their life of wrongdoing.

They may resent being bothered at first, but if I have enough love, I will keep trying to awaken them by sharing God's love.

Love your neighbor as yourself. (Luke 10:27)

Give me enough love, O Lord, to want to share with my neighbor what I have experienced. Thank you for your sustaining love. Amen.

How do you best show love?

False Prophets　　　September 23

While visiting a wax museum, I was often not sure if a person was real or just made of wax. The artists of the wax figures made them look so lifelike that I smiled at the guard, only to realize, when he didn't smile back, that he was a wax figure.

Jesus said that's how false prophets are. They look like something they're not. Not everyone who speaks of god has necessarily been sent by God.

Watch out for false prophets. They come to you in sheep's clothing, but inwardly they are ferocious wolves. (Matt. 7:15)

Thank you, Jesus, for your words of warning. Give me direction in discerning words of truth. Amen.

Be discerning about what you hear.

By Their Fruit　　　September 24

I studied many figures in the wax museum. I had learned that I couldn't be sure they were real people until I saw them move or speak.

So it is with false prophets. I can't be sure people are prophets of God until I observe Christlike qualities in them. Blindly following anyone who claims to be from God is unwise. I must learn to test what I hear with what I know from the Scriptures. The responsibility is mine to question whether or not a prophet has the fruit of living under the lordship of Christ.

By their fruit you will recognize them. (Matt. 7:16)

Remind me, Jesus, to always question what kind of fruit a prophet has before blindly following. Thank you for your guidance. Amen.

Evaluate the "fruit" in the lives of the spiritual leaders you respect.

Sunshine Makes Shadows
September 25

A friend told me of an experience she had while flying above the clouds in an airplane. The sun was shining brightly around her, but when she looked down between the clouds, she noticed that the clouds were blocking the sun. Even though the sun was shining above, the people below couldn't see it. The clouds under the sun produced dark shadows on the ground.

When dark times come, instead of complaining about the clouds that cause the shadows, I need to realize that the sun is still shining beyond the clouds. Sunshine sometimes produces shadows to bring awareness of its light.

I have learned the secret of being content in any and every situation, whether well fed or hungry, whether living in plenty or in want. (Phil. 4:12)

Thank you, Lord, for your light. When it produces shadows in my life, teach me to realize that sunshine is near— just beyond the clouds. Amen.

What kind of sky and clouds are above you today?

———————————————

God Is Dependable   September 26

Wondering how many times a day children call on their parents, I listened closely to the activities of our home for one day. I heard everything from "Mom, where's my shirt?" to "Dad, will you take me shopping?" with countless other emergencies in between. We knew without thinking about it that our parents would listen and help in the best way they knew how.

God is even more dependable than my earthly parents; he is always ready to listen and answer my prayers. All I need to do is ask. I can learn to talk to God as naturally as I talk to the people with whom I live.

If you, then, though you are evil, know how to give good gifts to your children, how much more will your Father in heaven give good gifts to those who ask him! (Matt. 7:11)

God, thank you for always being near and hearing my prayers. May I learn to talk to you more naturally throughout my daily tasks. Amen.

Think of God once a minute for the next fifteen minutes.

———————————————

God's Love Continues   September 27

Another thing I have discovered about the parent-child relationship is that most of the time it's the child who is asking for something. If the parents do something right, they are usually left without a word of praise. But if they do something wrong, they're sure to be reminded of it. Amazingly, their love continues.

Too often I communicate with my heavenly Father only when something goes wrong. I forget to thank him for a job well done. It's amazing how God's love for me continues when I keep asking for more and forget to say, "I love you."

I love the Lord because he hears my prayers and answers them. (Ps. 116:1 LB)

Forgive me, Lord, when I continually ask for things and forget to thank you for them. I love you. Amen.

How has God answered one of your prayers this week?

———◆—◆—◆———

Choosing Friends   September 28

High school was a time when I made social breaks from my family and began to spend more time with other people. Some people seem easier to get to know than others, but to really know anyone takes time.

One particular friend and I knew each other a year before we could share our real feelings. She had always reminded me of the typical all-American teen-ager—happy, efficient, always ready to shop, good looking, from a nice family, etc. As we grew closer, however, I realized that she had her share of rough times, too.

The true riches in life are found in really knowing people and sharing with them my deepest convictions. My choice of friends will determine the kind of life I live.

A mirror reflects a man's face, but what he is really like is shown by the kind of friends he chooses. (Prov. 27:19 LB)

Jesus, guide me in choosing my friends—ones who bring me closer to you. May I be the kind of friend to others that you want me to be. Amen.

What does your choice of friends say about you?

———————————————

Lonely People   September 29

There was a nursing home just down the road from where I lived, so some friends and I took the opportunity to visit some of its lonely residents. Glenn, the man I chose to visit, was ninety-four years old and spent most of his time in bed.

Some weeks when I went to his room, he told me stories of his past. Sometimes he complained about his failing health. At other times we enjoyed sitting together in silence. Each time, when I stood to leave, he told me how much my visits meant to him.

What we talked about wasn't as important to him as knowing someone cared about him. I'll never be sorry for the time I've spent with this lonely person.

The king will answer them, "Truly I tell you, just as you did it to one of the least of these who are members of my family, you did it to me." (Matt. 25:40 NRSV)

Thank you, Lord, for the opportunities I have to be a friend to lonely people. I pray that I will make use of these times to spread your love and care. Amen.

Visit a lonely person.

———————————————

Sad in Love   September 30

*My newest griefs to Thee are old;
My last transgression of Thy law,*

Though wrapped in thought's most secret fold,
Thine eyes with pitying sadness saw.

These words of H. M. Kimball portray a God of compassion. When I sin, God isn't angry, thinking of revenge. God is sad, thinking only of love.

When I sin, I almost wish God would be harsh. Then I'd feel I got what I deserved. But God is love, and in responding love I want to do only that which makes God happy.

May my spoken words and unspoken thoughts be pleasing even to you, O Lord, my Rock and my Redeemer. (Ps. 19:14 LB)

Forgive me, my Redeemer, for the times I've made you sad. I want to do only what makes you happy. Amen.

Do a deed that you know will make God happy.

MICHAEL SILUK

Flexibility Needed   October 1

I once heard someone say that the reason the Constitution of the United States has been useful for so long is that it is tremendously flexible. That statement reminded me that in our changing world, my mind needs to be flexible to be useful as well.

The Bible never changes, but I must always read it with a mind open to change in myself. God will reveal the truth to me if my mind is flexible enough to hear any new directions above my own stubborn beliefs and wrongdoings.

I am listening carefully to all the Lord is saying—for he speaks peace to his people, his saints, if they will only stop their sinning. (Ps. 85:8 LB)

Thank you, God, for the stability of your Word. Give me an attitude of flexibility that is willing to change when you show me a new truth. Amen.

Where is God asking for flexibility in you?

Always More   October 2

I like the story in 1 Kings of the woman who had enough faith to feed Elijah her last handful of flour and last drops of oil, even though she and her son faced starvation. Because she obeyed God, she received as much as she needed. Her flour and oil never ran out.

I have never known what it is to have as little as this woman, but I wonder if I'd be as willing to give as she was. It's sometimes hard to give, even out of my plenty. This story teaches a powerful lesson. Even if God's commands don't always seem sensible, those who obey are rewarded.

For no matter how much they used, there was always plenty left in the containers, just as the Lord had promised through Elijah! (1 Kings 17:16 LB)

Lord, thank you for all that you've given to me. Grant that I will always be willing to give even if it means less for me. Amen.

Give away a treasured possession.

———————◆——◆◆——◆◆———————

Leaves and Other Blessings
October 3

Last fall I received a letter from a friend who has lived in the deserts of Arizona. He told me of a weekend retreat he had attended in the distant Rocky Mountains. The highlight of the weekend for him seemed to be seeing the beauty of the red, orange, and yellow autumn leaves and hearing them crunch underfoot.

Because I had lived in the mountains of Virginia, the fall leaves were commonplace for me, and many times as I had shuffled through them, I hardly noticed their beauty. My friend's letter reminded me of the many gifts God has provided for my enjoyment.

I want to express publicly before his people my heartfelt thanks to God for his mighty miracles. All who are thankful should ponder them with me. (Ps. 111:1–2 LB)

Thank you, Lord, for beautiful autumn leaves and the many other blessings you have given me, waiting only for my appreciation. Amen.

Discover the ordinary things of your world anew!

———————◆——◆◆——◆◆———————

God Waits
October 4

Hearing the crunch of dried leaves under my feet, feeling the crisp wind nip my nose as it rushes by, and watching the squirrels gather acorns for the winter are only a few of the signs of autumn that put excitement in the air. It's as if nature has a secret that she whispers to anyone who is willing to stop and listen.

That reminds me of the way God speaks. Excitement fills the air when I recognize God's presence in the things and people around me—when I wait and listen for the secrets whispered in the quiet. Not only in autumn, but every day of the year, I can hear God's voice.

Come near to God and he will come near to you. (James 4:8)

Thank you, God, for your patience. Grant me awareness of your waiting voice when I forget to stop and listen. Amen.

Listen to the whispers of your heart.

Look Straight Ahead
October 5

Watching a horse pull a cart along the road, I noticed that blinders had been fastened on its bridle so it could only see straight ahead. The blinders prevented the horse from being distracted by activities at the sides.

Sometimes I think it might be good if I could attach something to my eyes too, to prevent me from being distracted along the road to eternal life. It's often tempting to look behind or beside me instead of keeping my eyes on God. To reach my goal, I must only look forward and keep moving in that direction.

Submit yourselves, then, to God. Resist the devil, and he will flee from you. (James 4:7)

Lord, help me to continue to look to you, even when distractions are tempting me to go in another direction. Thank you for leading me. Amen.

Let God fasten your blinders!

Turning the Other Cheek

October 6

As a child, I remember times when one of us children would put on the "holier than thou" attitude for a while and turn the other cheek instead of hitting back. We were taking Matthew 5:39 literally. The rest would take advantage of the offer and hit the other cheek too! I believe Jesus had more meaning in those words than I understood then. He wanted to teach the proper attitude to have toward those who hurt me. I must be willing to take hurt without wishing anything bad to happen to the one who hurt me. With Jesus' help, I can forgive without thought of retaliation.

But I tell you, Do not resist an evil person. If someone strikes you on the right cheek, turn to him the other also. (Matt. 5:39)

Forgive me, Jesus, for the times when I haven't taken hurt without retaliation as you told me to. Help me to be more sensitive to your Spirit. Amen.

What's an act of love that can be an alternative to retaliation?

Soar High   October 7

A rare species of cormorants live on the Galapagos Islands. They have wings, but they can't fly. They have no enemies to fly from, and they can obtain their food on foot, so they have no need to fly.

This creature is typical of some people. By failing to use their God-given abilities, they refuse to soar in the spiritual realm. By remaining in secular society, they forget the beauty and excitement of lifting their lives to higher and better experiences.

Do not neglect your gift. (1 Tim. 4:14)

Thank you, dear God, for abilities you have given to me. Teach me to use them so I don't lose them. Amen.

Revive an unused gift.

Using Available Tools   October 8

Another animal on the Galapagos Islands is a small bird called the woodpecker finch. Its distinguishing feature is that it is one of the few living creatures, besides humans, that use a tool. It digs insects out of holes with twigs that it breaks off trees.

The woodpecker finch is typical of some people. It has learned to use tools that are available for survival. Similarly, many people use the tools of learning for personal growth. God helps me grow when I make use of what I already have.

Be diligent in these matters; give yourself wholly to them, so that everyone may see your progress. (1 Tim. 4:15)

Teach me, Lord, to recognize the tools available to me to use in my personal growth. Amen.

Loving the Stranger — October 9

As I jumped out of the car, engulfed in my plans for the day ahead, I heard a "Good morning!" I looked up to see a man waving at me from across the lawn. His hair was disheveled, and his belly stuck out between his sloppy pants and open shirt—the kind of person I knew my friends would laugh at and disregard as "crazy." But I waved back, noticing his smile and enjoyment of the day. I thought, *That's a person to whom Jesus would say, "Good morning!" And I smiled, infected by his carefree joy.*

Whatever you did for one of the least of these brothers of mine, you did for me. (Matt. 25:40).

Jesus, help me to be more welcoming to the strangers I meet. Remind me of how you love them. Amen.

Infect others with your joy.

A New House — October 10

A house in our neighborhood was so run-down and dilapidated that no one wanted to live in it. Then a couple decided to buy it and fix it up. They saw hope in what others saw only as ruin. When they finished remodeling, the house looked like new.

My life is like that house. Before I gave it to Christ, it was torn up and on its way to being ruined by sin. But when I gave Christ the ownership, I was transformed into a new person. I pray that Christ will continue making repairs, adding new rooms, and making any other necessary improvements on my "house."

Listen! I am standing at the door, knocking; if you hear my voice and open the door, I will come in to you and eat with you, and you with me. (Rev. 3:20 NRSV)

I'm so happy you saw something worth fixing in my life, O Christ, instead of giving me up as hopeless. Thank you for all the work you're doing in me. Amen.

What "room" is Christ remodeling in you?

———— •• —••— •• ————

Freedom to Choose   October 11

Sometimes when I pray for the salvation of one of my friends, God doesn't seem to be answering. I want some immediate miracle so my friend will desire only to know and serve God.

God, however, doesn't manipulate anyone's life. Instead of controlling me like a puppet, he gives me freedom to choose. God will help me influence others with my life, but I can make decisions only for myself. I must, therefore, ask God to guide me in ways of showing love to those around me.

This is right and is acceptable in the sight of God our Savior, who desires everyone to be saved and to come to the knowledge of the truth. (1 Tim. 2:3–4 NRSV)

O mighty God, I realize that even though you want all people to be saved, you don't manipulate them. Show me ways I can be an effective influence for you. Amen.

Pray for a non-Christian friend and know that's the most powerful thing you can do.

———— •• —••— •• ————

Bloom Where You
Are Planted   October 12

"Bloom where you are planted." Those words were proclaimed from the showcase at school in big, colorful letters. They were a beautiful reminder of my responsibility to be happy in whatever situation I am placed.

When I'm planted in happy surroundings, it's easy to bloom; but tense and tough situations make it difficult. Nevertheless, the words remain: "Bloom where you are planted." The challenge isn't to bloom only when I'm planted in easy situations but to continue blooming in hard surroundings as well.

As servants of God we commend ourselves in every way: in great endurance; in troubles, hardships and distresses. (2 Cor. 6:4)

Thank you, Lord, for giving me strength to bloom wherever I'm planted. May I continue to draw nourishment from you. Amen.

Give a flower.

Sharing Troubles   October 13

When my younger brother was taken to the hospital for several days, God's love shone through to our family in many ways. Friends and neighbors brought meals to us, took some of my parents' responsibilities, and assured us of their prayers. They truly shared our troubles, as Paul commended the Philippians for sharing his. Because I knew how much we appreciated their help, it became an incentive to me to share the troubles of others in material ways and in prayer.

Yet it was good of you to share in my troubles. (Phil. 4:14)

Thank you, Lord, for brothers and sisters who follow your way of sharing my troubles. They make you more real. Amen.

Assure a sick person of your prayers.

The Intercessor   October 14

Sometimes people get facts mixed up when they're praying, and I find myself correcting them in my mind. Usually I know what they mean, but they probably don't realize what they have said. It makes me wonder how often I don't realize how I'm praying and thus ask for the wrong things.

It's a blessing to know that when I want to follow God's will, the Holy Spirit intercedes for me and straightens out my prayers. The Spirit understands thoughts I can't express in words and tells God my desires and praise. The Spirit makes it possible for me to speak to God with wisdom.

We do not know what we ought to pray for, but the Spirit himself intercedes for us with groans that words cannot express. (Rom. 8:26)

Dear Father, thank you for your Holy Spirit, who intercedes for me and knows how to pray when I don't. Amen.

Without words, meditate on who God is.

Complete Trust   October 15

Much is said in the Bible about Paul of Tarsus, before and after his conversion. But it's easy to overlook Ananias, the man whose faith was used to save Paul.

When Ananias was sent to talk to Paul about God, Paul was a dangerous man, with authority to arrest Christians. In spite of these dangers, Ananias put his trust completely in God and obeyed. Because of this, God was able to do a great thing through him. His example is an inspiring one, showing me how much God can do through me when I trust him completely.

In Damascus there was a disciple named Ananias. The Lord called to him in a vision, "Ananias!" "Yes, Lord," he answered. (Acts 9:10).

Thank you, God, for examples of people of great faith like Ananias. Help me to have more faith. Amen.

Sing a song about faith.

———————◆━━━◆━━━◆————————

No Disagreement   October 16

I listened as two people talked to each other. They were growing quite upset because to each of them the other seemed to be stubborn and rude. Hearing both sides, I soon realized that neither was hearing correctly what the other was saying. When I asked each to say what he was hearing the other person say, they laughed at themselves. The serious misunderstanding had come from the smaller misunderstanding of each individual. When each knew what the other had really said, there was no more disagreement.

That situation made me wonder how often I become upset with people merely because I don't hear what they're really saying. Maybe if I'd be more careful to listen well, many disagreements would disappear.

Do not judge, and you will not be judged. Do not condemn, and you will not be condemned. Forgive, and you will be forgiven. (Luke 6:37)

Lord, guide me through each day and each conversation. I pray that I will try to understand others rather than being quick to judge them. Amen.

Pray for listening power.

———————————

The Joy of Living   October 17

I have a friend who always looks happy. She seems to enjoy every moment of life and makes experiences that would be boring for others fresh with excitement. As we became closer friends, I realized that she was an ordinary person, with extraordinary faith.

With Jesus, it is possible to make every day an exciting adventure. I am challenged by each experience to show my faith through the joy of living.

So I say to you: Ask and it will be given to you; seek and you will find; knock and the door will be opened to you. (Luke 11:9)

Teach me, Lord, to respond to everyday experiences with a fresh attitude. Thank you for providing a reason to be joyful. Amen.

Today is a new day to begin life again!

———————————

A Half-Baked Life   October 18

Trying a new cake recipe turned into a disaster. After the cake was baked and cooled, it looked good, but when it was cut open, it lost its attraction. The inside was a mass of heavy, soggy dough. I hadn't baked it long enough.

Unless I live according to God's "recipe" each day, I am not fully ready to serve. What my life looks like on the outside isn't necessarily what it is on the inside until God has total control over me.

My people mingle with the heathen, picking up their evil ways; thus they become as good-for-nothing as a half-baked cake! (Hos. 7:8 LB)

Lord, help me to "bake" evenly so the inside is as good as the outside looks. Thank you for living in me. Amen.

Look in the mirror. Does your inside match your outside?

Strength to Pedal   October 19

Riding my bicycle through the hills around my home has provided many hours of enjoyment. The hard work of pedaling up the hills is rewarded by the fun of flying downhill with little effort. When I reach the bottom, however, I must begin with renewed energy to tackle the next climb. If I coast until the bike slows down, it's harder to regain momentum.

When life is easy, I sometimes forget that hard times may lie ahead. I coast without thinking about renewing my strength for the next climb. But I am given the assurance that God will help renew my energy and give me purpose in the climbs.

You need to persevere so that when you have done the will of God, you will receive what he has promised. (Heb. 10:36)

Thank you, God, for helping me gain momentum on the "down-hills" of life to help me up the next hill. Give me strength when the hills become long and hard. Amen.

Are you pedaling or coasting today?

The Psalm of the Good Teacher

The Lord is my Teacher;
I shall not lose my way to wisdom.
He leadeth me in the lowly path of learning,
He prepareth a lesson for me every day.
He findeth the clear fountain of instruction—
Little by little He showeth me the beauty of truth.
The world is a great book that He has written,
He turneth the leaves for me slowly;
They are inscribed with images and letters—
His voice poureth light on the pictures and the words.
Then am I glad when I perceive His meaning.
He taketh me by the hand to the hilltop of wisdom;
In the valley, also, He walketh beside me,
And in the dark places He whispereth in my heart.
Yea, though my lesson be hard, it is not hopeless,
For the Lord is very patient with His slow scholar.
He will wait for my weakness—
He will help me to read the truth through tears—
Surely Thou wilt enlighten me daily by joy and by sorrow,
And lead me at last, O Lord, to the perfect knowledge of Thee.

—Henry van Dyke

Because the Lord is my Shepherd, I have everything I need! (Ps. 23:1 LB)

Thank you for being my Teacher and Lord. I give the difficulty of my lessons over to you. Please help me with them. Amen.

Write down a recent lesson from your heavenly Teacher.

Pass It On

I have a friend who loves to do things for other people, and she doesn't seem to expect anything in return. When it's impossible for me to repay her acts of kindness, she tells me to do something for someone else, and that will be pay enough.

She is a beautiful example of the kind of love Christ has for me. I can never repay Jesus for what he's done for me, but I can show my gratitude by spreading his love to others.

Jesus told him, "Go and do likewise." (Luke 10:37)

Your love, O Christ, is more than I can repay except by telling others about it. Thank you for your amazing love. Amen.

Give someone a backrub.

The Mighty God

When I reached the top of a mountain with a group of friends, we broke into songs of praise to God. The view was beautiful as we looked down on miles of trees and up into the clear blue sky. Seeing the earth from high above made us feel especially close to God.

After seeing all this beauty and majesty in creation, I saw myself as only a tiny part of God's vast purpose on earth. I felt the great privilege of having God, who made all that I saw, as my personal Savior.

My help is from Jehovah who made the mountains! And the heavens too! (Ps. 121:2 LB)

O mighty Savior, I thank you for caring about me amid all the grandeur of your creation. Thank you for the beauty all around me. Amen.

See the beauty of a tree.

Communication Techniques   October 23

Not only can words make a friendship; they can also break a friendship. For this reason God gives rules for their use. Many such rules are found in the book of James.

Listening takes time, but it's usually time well spent. Too often I don't listen enough but speak too quickly. Unwise words are a powerful tool of destruction, often leading to anger. Consideration in communicating involves carefully weighing my words and the words of others.

You must understand this, my beloved: let everyone be quick to listen, slow to speak, slow to anger. (James 1:19 NRSV)

Teach me, O God, to be more sensitive to others in my words, silences, and actions. Thank you for being patient with me when I fail. Amen.

Listen today at least as much as you talk.

Unrecognized Honor   October 24

Often it's hardest to see good things in people I've known the longest. I think I know them so well that I no longer try to see new actions or talents they may have.

Jesus is a good example. Although he was the Son of God and did many miracles, the people of Nazareth didn't accept him. Knowing his earthly parents, they couldn't believe he was greater than anyone else.

It is only in looking at those I know in a new light every day that I can see their abilities as God see them.

Jesus said to them, "Only in his home town, among his relatives and in his own house is a prophet without honor." (Mark 6:4)

Prevent me, Lord, from failing to see the virtues of those near me. Help me to always look for the good in others. Amen.

Notice a new gift in your best friend.

———◆◆◆———◆◆———

The Difficulty of
Self-Forgiveness   October 25

From a recent experience, I've discovered that sometimes it's harder to forgive myself than for the person I've wronged to forgive me. Once when I tried to play a joke on a friend, it turned out to be a painful experience for him. After I talked to him about it, he forgave me, but the stupidity of my thoughtlessness bothered me for days.

God said our sins are taken so far away that we can never find them again. With this promise, I don't have to let guilt haunt my mind after I've been forgiven. I can learn to forgive myself because God has forgiven me, and I can go on from there.

He has removed our sins as far away from us as the east is from the west. (Ps. 103:12 LB)

Thank you, God, for your forgiving Spirit. Teach me to forgive myself too. Amen.

Imagine God's forgiveness covering you from head to toe.

———◆◆———◆◆———◆◆———

Know the Work October 26

Lured by the glory football players receive after a good game, one of my friends decided to join the team one year. After a week of hard practice, he quit. He hadn't realized how tough the work was.

The same thing can happen in my life if I look at the gloriousness of life in Christ and miss the hardships. Jesus makes it clear that his way isn't the easiest. I must not let my enthusiasm block out the cost of discipleship but always be willing to be a hard worker.

Jesus replied, "Foxes have holes and birds of the air have nests, but the Son of Man has no place to lay his head." (Luke 9:58)

Your way, O Lord, may not be the easiest, but it is the most worthwhile. I want to continue following you. Amen.

Think about the ways in which following Jesus makes life harder.

God Shines Through October 27

The sun comes up every morning whether I notice it or not. It provides light for me and makes my food grow even if I don't always appreciate it.

Like the sun, God shines into my life each day, and over the whole world. I can enjoy life much more when I don't become too busy to notice or appreciate God's light and warmth shining on me and on all the rest of creation.

Let everything he has made give praise to him. (Ps. 148:5 LB)

Almighty God, grant that I will never take your shining love for granted, but that I may look anew each day at the great privilege of knowing you. I praise you, for you are a great God. Amen.

Let light be a reminder to you of God's promises.

Jesus as the Guide   October 28

One day Dad was driving along a highway behind a truck. As the truck turned off onto a side road, Dad followed. By the time he realized his mistake, a whole string of cars were following him too!

It's easy to be led astray by others without giving it much thought. Jesus came into the world to save those who are lost and to lead them back to the right way. I must continually look to him to show me the way and not be ignorantly distracted by the direction others take.

And I, the Messiah, came to save the lost. (Matt. 18:11 LB)

Thank you, Jesus, for showing me the way. Prevent me from following others merely because they seem to be going the way I'm going. Amen.

Do your plans include Jesus' direction?

Free from Sin   October 29

After a heavy rain, my brother and I went for a walk. When we came to a bank that was covered with mud, my brother slid down it on his feet. It looked like fun, and I couldn't resist. When I slid down, however, I fell, twisted my arm, and pulled a muscle. Seeing only the pleasure, I hadn't anticipated the pain that followed.

Sinful ways sometimes look attractive too. They don't look harmful at first, but if I yield, unexpected results take place. Christ knows the deceitful ways of sin and wants to set me free from sin's trap.

You have been set free from sin and have become slaves to righteousness. (Rom. 6:18)

Thank you, Lord, for freeing me from sin and its cunning ways of deception. Guide me in the way of righteousness. Amen.

Who or what enslaves you?

God Is   October 30

Is it possible to believe there is no God? I don't see how. In the words of Nikita Ivanovich Panin, "The world we inhabit must have had an origin; that origin must have consisted in a cause; that cause must have been intelligent; that intelligence must have been supreme; and that supreme, which always was and is supreme, we know by the name of God."

One God and Father of all, who is over all and through all and in all. (Eph. 4:6)

Thank you, God, for your supreme intelligence that caused the origin of the world. I will praise your name forever. Amen.

Think of five ways God gives meaning to your world.

Closeness Counts   October 31

From the many tours I've been on, I know the importance of staying near the guide. When I wander off by myself or lag behind, I miss all the facts the guide is relating.

When I wander, following my own desires and interests, I can no longer hear what Jesus is saying either, and I become frustrated. Only by staying as near to his leading as possible can I be sure I'm hearing all that he says to me.

If you are willing and obedient, you will eat the best from the land. (Isa. 1:19)

Jesus, thank you for being the Guide of my life. Grant that I will always stay close enough to hear you. Amen.

List the ways in which you are rich.

CLEO FREELANCE PHOTO

Enjoying Laziness   November 1

An article entitled "How to Be Lazy—and Love It" caught my attention. I don't usually have a problem with laziness, but when I am sometimes lazy, it's hard to enjoy it without feeling guilty. I was amused and helped by the following suggestions:

Be too lazy to frown, fidget, or fuss.

Listen more than you talk.

Don't bother quarreling over insignificant things.

Don't knock yourself out for a bargain that takes more out of you than it saves the piggy bank.

Be too lazy to worry your mind with the inevitable.

This is the best way I have found to be lazy and love it. Those close to me also enjoy this kind of laziness in me.

O Israel, you too should quietly trust in the Lord— now, and always. (Ps. 131:3 LB)

Thank you, Lord, for these directions for being lazy. Help me put them into practice. Amen.

Be lazy.

Nothing Can Be Hidden   November 2

Cleaning my room for a friend's visit one day, I didn't have time to put everything away, so I threw some things under the bed. They were out of sight, but not out of my mind. Later, I took them out and put them where they belonged.

This incident made me think of how I sometimes try to block things out of my mind—hurting others, a cutting remark, or my insensitivity to someone's needs. I may be able to hide my wrong for a while, but it will never disappear completely until I make it right.

There is nothing concealed that will not be disclosed, or hidden that will not be made known. (Matt. 10:26)

Forgive me, Lord, for times when I've tried to ignore things I've done wrong. Thank you for helping me to see the necessity of correcting them. Amen.

What's been left "under your bed"?

Hang On   *November 3*

I like the story of a girl who dreamed that she died and went to heaven. Seeing her name on a box in the corner marked "Prayer Requests," she asked an angel what it was. The angel said that when God's children make a request, the answer is prepared, but if the petitioner is not waiting for it, it is returned and stored in this corner.

Waiting is difficult, but it is not in vain if we wait expectantly and patiently. An old proverb says, "When you come to the end of your rope, tie a prayer knot and hang on."

But if we hope for what we do not yet have, we wait for it patiently. (Rom. 8:25)

Lord, grant that I will have expectancy when I pray and the patience to hang on and wait. Amen.

For what answer to prayer do you wait?

Different Formations   November 4

A lump of dirty coal and a beautiful, glimmering diamond don't seem to have many similarities, but both are composed of nearly the same elements. The difference is in the way they were formed.

People are quite different from one another, too, although we are basically the same. Each person was made in God's image. The difference is in the formation. When I give my life to Christ, I am molded into a new person. Instead of having bad thoughts about others, I can remember that the only difference between us is the way in which we were formed.

"For the LORD does not see as mortals see; they look on the outward appearance, but the LORD looks on the heart." (1 Sam. 16:7 NRSV)

Thank you, God, for forming my life. I want to continually give myself to you for your molding. Amen.

Place a jewel beside a lump of coal or dirt to remind you of your Creator.

Slow Down   November 5

"Take it easy. Slow down. Think about what you're doing." Those are the familiar words of our basketball coach when we become tense in a game and make careless mistakes.

It's good advice for the rest of life as well. God wants me to put forth my best efforts but, at the same time, to slow down enough to enjoy them. If I can enjoy the process as much as the finished goals, life stays fresh with a deep joy and peace.

He will keep in perfect peace all those who trust in him, whose thoughts turn often to the Lord! (Isa. 26:3 LB)

Thank you, Jesus, my Coach, for directing my game of life. If I step out of your timing, help me to slow down. Amen.

Are you enjoying this moment?

Spiritual Strength   November 6

Doctors say that most people don't use their full physical strength, though several stories have been told of people who used extraordinary strength in emergencies, such as lifting a car to save a person's life. Psychologists also say that we use only a fraction of our mental abilities—abilities apparently available for our use if we but knew how to tap them.

The same is probably true of spiritual powers. If I were warned about each experience before it happened, I might not think I have enough strength to handle it. But each time, God provides enough power to face the new situation.

I pray also that the eyes of your heart may be enlightened in order that you may know the hope to which he has called you, the riches of his glorious inheritance in the saints, and his incomparably great power for us who believe. (Eph. 1:18–19)

Thank you, God, for giving me your special strength in every situation we face together. Continue to be my power. Amen.

How many times in the past week have you relied on God's strength?

Look Ahead

My mother tells me that after I buy something, I shouldn't look at the same thing in another store. I might have made the worst bargain, but because it's too late to change, I'll feel better by not comparing.

The same principle is true throughout life. Continually comparing the present to the past, wishing I had done something different, brings discontentment. The only thing I have control over is what I do now. Worrying about the past doesn't change anything, and by giving my past failures to God, I can go on with a lighter load.

But one thing I do: Forgetting what is behind and straining toward what is ahead, I press on. . . . (Phil. 3:13–14)

Help me to look ahead, Lord, and do what I can instead of regretting the past, which I can't change. Thank you for loving me in spite of all my past failures. Amen.

What regret is burdening you?

Courtesy

An unknown author wrote, "I am a little thing with a big meaning. I help unlock doors, open hearts, and dispel prejudice. I create friendships and good will. I inspire respect and admiration. Everybody loves me. I bore nobody. I violate no law. I cost nothing. Many have praised me; no one has condemned me. I am useful every moment of the day in many ways. I am called courtesy."

Finally, all of you, have unity of spirit, sympathy, love for one another, a tender heart, and a humble mind. (1 Peter 3:8 NRSV)

Jesus, help me to be courteous to everyone with whom I come in contact. Thank you for your example of courtesy. Amen.

Read the story of Jesus' being courteous to the Samaritan woman in John 4:1−26.

The Meaning of Discipleship
November 9

In Greek, the word for disciple means "learner" and carries with it the idea of discipline. Jesus, however, uses it with a much deeper meaning. He taught the need of total commitment of one's life to his authority if one would be his disciple. I can be a true disciple of Jesus' only when I'm willing to put my own desires aside for Christ's higher ways.

To the Jews who had believed him, Jesus said, "If you hold to my teaching, you are really my disciples." (John 8:31)

Thank you, Jesus, that it is possible to be your disciple. Guide me in everything I do that I will remain under your authority. Amen.

To what step of discipleship is Christ calling you today?

Unknown Waters
November 10

A friend and I were canoeing down a river when we decided to stop and hike on land for a while. Upon returning to the place where we had tied our canoe, we found that some friends had taken it to the other side as a joke! We were helpless without it, so we started across. We found, too late, that what looked like a beautiful, peaceful river from the shore had a strong, turbulent current beneath the surface that threatened to pull us under. With a struggle and a prayer, we eventually made it to the other side.

That river reminds me of some things in life. From a distance, they look safe, but when I become involved, the opposite is true. When I pray before venturing into unknown waters, many extra struggles are eliminated.

Humble yourselves, therefore, under God's mighty hand, that he may lift you up in due time. (1 Peter 5:6)

Thank you, Lord, for helping me out of the troubled waters I sometimes get caught in. Guide me in the future to be more careful of what I step into. Amen.

Imagine crossing a dangerous stream while holding Jesus' hand.

Work at Love   November 11

It's easy to think of love as a beautiful relationship that suddenly springs forth. As in a storybook romance, things fall together, and two people live happily ever after. But like a flower that blooms only after much cultivation and care, love also takes work. Instead of *falling* in love, I must *grow* in love.

In the same way, following Jesus with a deep, increasing expression of his love in my life does not just happen. I must work at becoming his disciple. I must follow him day by day to learn how to love him more and share his love with others.

Then he said to them all: "If any want to become my followers, let them deny themselves and take up their cross daily and follow me." (Luke 9:23 NRSV)

Give me patience, Lord, to work at becoming your disciple
just as I must work at everything else that's worthwhile. Amen.

Take a step of love.

━━━◆◆━━━◆━━━◆◆━━━

Take a Close Look   November 12

One day in a science class we looked at flowers under a microscope. The beauty of each intricate part of what had previously been an ordinary-looking flower was impossible to describe. Each person had to look personally to experience the joy. Since then I have recognized more beauty in each flower I see, because I know more of what's there.

Jesus, in glory, is that way too. Each person must also take the time to discover Jesus' true beauty personally. No words can do justice to the real picture of what life with Christ is like. Once people see Christ's glory, they only regret that they had not known it before.

The Word became flesh and made his dwelling among us. We have seen his glory, the glory of the One and Only, who came from the Father, full of grace and truth. (John 1:14)

Thank you, Jesus, for making yourself available for everyone to see. Grant that I will encourage others to discover your true beauty also. Amen.

Meditate on the intricate beauty of God's creation by looking closely at a flower.

━━━◆◆━━━◆━━━◆◆━━━

Life—A Book   November 13

In an article, "If I were 17 Again . . . and Know What I Know at 80," Josephine Fox Fink writes: "At 17 life is like a beautiful book in a gorgeous binding, but with blank pages you fill in from day to day in your life. I would try to live so that there would be no pages that I would want to skip over or tear out. Others would be pages to laugh about when I recalled them, and of course there would be sad pages, but they would be few and far between."

I like that. I like to think of life as a book of empty pages and that God has created me to choose what will be printed on those pages. It is a great privilege and responsibility—one I cannot fulfill alone.

You alone are my God; my times are in your hands. (Ps. 31:14–15 LB)

God, thank you for life, and thank you that you promised to be with me to enable me to choose and do what makes life beautiful. Amen.

What will you write on your next page?

Angels Today   November 14

A friend and I were standing at the top of a hill one evening, looking over the lights below. Suddenly, a man walked out from the shadows and began talking to us. He said that many of the people around that hill don't know Jesus, but those who do know him don't seem to have time to tell others about him. Therefore many would continue to live in darkness.

When he descended again into the shadows, we felt we had been visited by one of God's angels. Even though our visitor looked like an ordinary person, we felt God had sent him to deliver that message. I must always be listening for God's voice, no matter how it is sent.

As they talked and discussed these things with each other, Jesus himself came up and walked along

with them; but they were kept from recognizing him. (Luke 24:15–16)

Thank you, Lord, for sending angels today too. May I always be listening for what you are saying to me through your messengers. Amen.

What personal message would an angel from God have for you?

A Little at a Time   November 15

"The best way to get much done is to always be doing a little." Those were the words on a plaque at school. I thought about them when the amount of work to be done seemed so huge that I hardly knew where to start. I learned that the best way to deal with that is to start somewhere and not think about the rest until there's time to do it. Surprisingly enough, things get done faster that way than when I worry about them. Thinking only of what I'm doing now makes a project more enjoyable than if I only think of it in the context of all that remains to be done.

Therefore do not worry about tomorrow, for tomorrow will worry about itself. Each day has enough trouble of its own. (Matt. 6:34)

Thank you for helping me get things done, Lord, and for the knowledge that I don't need to spend time worrying about them. Amen.

Make a list of all you have to do and cross out each item as it is completed.

Pointing Back at Me   November 16

As a child, when I was questioned about some wrong-doing, it wasn't unusual for me to point at one of my brothers or my sister, trying to redirect the blame. It also wasn't unusual for one of them to say, "You have three fingers pointing back at yourself." I didn't like that reminder, but it was true.

Today when I point at others who do wrong, it's still true that I have three fingers pointing back at myself. After all the times God has forgiven me, how can I point at others for doing wrong? I can only ask God to forgive me.

When they kept on questioning him, he straightened up and said to them, "If any one of you is without sin, let him be the first to throw a stone at her." (John 8:7)

Forgive me, God, for pointing my finger too often and blaming others. Give me the strength to take my own responsibility. Amen.

Write a prayer of confession.

Take My Life   November 17

Take my life and let it be
Consecrated, Lord, to Thee;
Take my moments and my days:
Let them flow in ceaseless praise.

This song has deep meaning when I pray it sincerely from my heart as well as sing it with my mouth. I'm saying that every moment of every day is for God's use and that I will continually praise God. And why shouldn't I? Jesus bought me at a high price. By accepting him as my Lord, I consecrate my life to Christ.

You are not your own; you were bought at a price. Therefore honor God with your body. (1 Cor. 6:19–20)

My life, O Lord, is in your hands. Thank you for the joy of serving you. Amen.

Write God's assurance of pardon to the confession of yesterday's prayer.

———————◆◆——◆◆——◆———————

Serendipity
November 18

The word *serendipity* means the discovery of something good by accident. It comes from a story about the king of Serendip, who sent his sons on a journey. Since they were obedient and faithful, they discovered beautiful and valuable treasures all along the way.

My main goal today is to find the will of God and do it all along the way. Exciting surprises are planted in my path. I cannot foresee all that is in store for me. I can only praise God for what is continually provided.

But seek first his kingdom and his righteousness, and all these things will be given to you as well. (Matt. 6:33)

Thank you, Ruler of heaven and earth, for all the unexpected joy and happiness you provide for me. Amen.

Look for planted treasure in your path.

———————◆◆——◆◆——◆———————

Bought Twice November 19

At the end of each school year, an afternoon is set aside to give the students an opportunity to buy what has accumulated in the lost-and-found box. After an item is on the auctioning table, it's too late to claim it as lost. One of my friends recognized one of her shirts among the items and bought it back.

It didn't seem fair that she had to pay for the shirt twice. Neither does it seem fair that God had to pay twice for each one of us. I belong to God first because he created me, and second because I was bought with the blood of Jesus.

For you know that it was not with perishable things such as silver or gold that you were redeemed ... but with the precious blood of Christ. (1 Peter 1:18–19)

Thank you, Jesus, for your love, which was great enough to make me yours twice. Amen.

Contemplate Jesus dying for you.

———◆—◆———

Stay Alert November 20

The father of one of my friends is a volunteer fireman and policeman. In their home they have an instrument that announces any need for help. It stays on all the time, and as soon as help is called for, no matter what my friend's father is doing, he goes. He fully participates in all the activities at home, but he also keeps his ears open for any emergency directions.

As a follower of Jesus, I must have the same kind of built-in alertness and loyalty. In the midst of my everyday activities, I need to be constantly receptive to any directions the Holy Spirit sends me and be willing to act accordingly.

For all who are led by the Spirit of God are children of God. (Rom. 8:14 NRSV)

Thank you, God, for your Spirit, who gives me directions for my life. Thank you for giving me the desire to do your will. Grant that I will remain alert for your call. Amen.

What message might the Holy Spirit be sending you?

———————————

Imprisoned   November 21

With no jail near our house, I wondered how I could fulfill Christ's command to visit those in prison. I had read about prison conditions but had never been inside a prison.

Then I began to think about other kinds of prisons people are in—prisons of fear, insecurity, hatred, wealth, or stubbornness. Bars and keys aren't the only things that bind people. As Christ's messenger, I can visit them to tell of the freedom available to them. Jesus said that whatever I do for the least of these, it is as if I've done it for him.

I was in prison and you came to visit me. (Matt. 25:36)

Guide me, Lord, in doing your work—sharing with those who have become imprisoned by the miseries of life. Help me to know how to be a friend to them. Amen.

Look for the prison in which a friend might be bound.

———————————

Living for Others   November 22

When my brother returned from visiting friends, he brought with him a recipe for homemade bread. He liked the bread so well that he wanted to learn to make it himself. His first loaves weren't as good as those his friends had made, but he kept trying, and each time they turned out better. Soon our family thought his bread was better than any other kind.

Doing good deeds is like baking bread. The more often I do them, the easier they become. When it becomes natural to do things for others, I can no longer be satisfied with living only for myself.

Thieves must give up stealing; rather let them labor and work honestly with their own hands, so as to have something to share with the needy. (Eph. 4:28 NRSV)

Thank you, Lord, for the desire to do good deeds. Make them so much a part of my life that I would be uncomfortable not doing them. Amen.

Offer your services to someone who is too busy.

A Pile of Ashes   November 23

It was late in the fall when I went camping with a group of friends. The only source of heat in our cabin was a fireplace. Before we went to bed, we built a big fire, which we had hoped would last all night. In the morning, all that remained was a pile of ashes, but by blowing on the hot embers and putting small shavings of wood and pieces of paper on them, we soon rekindled the fire.

God probably sees my life as a pile of ashes sometimes. In the ashes of coming to the end of my own resources, Christ breathes new life into me and rekindles my flame. My fire does not only last for a night, but for all eternity.

Then Abraham spoke again. "Since I have begun, let
me go on and speak further to the Lord, though I
am but dust and ashes." (Gen. 18:27 LB)

*Thank you, Jesus, for the breath of your Spirit blowing in
me. Grant that my flame will always be kindled for your
ministry. Amen.*

Is your flame dying down or being rekindled?

Give Thanks — November 24

At our Thanksgiving dinner, each of us found five kernels
of corn on our plate. Before we began the meal, we were each
to think of five things—one for each kernel—that we were
thankful for. I kept those kernels on my desk for a long time
to remind myself of all that I have to be thankful for.
Thanksgiving isn't the only day to think of the many
blessings God has given me. Maybe this year I should think of
things for an entire corncob. I'm sure I wouldn't run out of
things for which I can be thankful.

Let every creature praise his holy name for ever
and ever. (Ps. 145:21)

*Thank you, God, for the many things you have given me
to be thankful for. I will praise your name forever. Amen.*

Be thankful throughout an entire meal.

Run the Race — November 25

As I watched the Olympics on television, I was awed by
the power, strength, and endurance—not only of the winners
but also of each participant. Pictures were shown of the hours

of training and hard work that preceded the competitions. The ones who received no recognition had been faithful in the difficult times just as those who received medals.

God has a prize for each one who perseveres in running the race of faith. Recognition for being the best runner isn't as important as the faithfulness to continue the race.

I have fought the good fight, I have finished the race, I have kept the faith. (2 Tim. 4:7)

Creator, give me strength and perseverance to do your will today. Help me to endure to the end. Amen.

What does your training consist of?

Active Good Will   November 26

"I don't love him any more. I'm filing for a divorce." "I don't love my parents. I'm going to live with someone else." These words have become too common in the world today. The word *love* has so many different meanings, it can be confusing.

The meaning of love as Paul writes of it in Ephesians, however, is different from a love based merely on feelings. It means "active good will." With God's help and my desire, I can exercise this kind of love. Christian love is lasting and stable.

And live a life of love, just as Christ loved us and gave himself up for us as a fragrant offering and sacrifice to God. (Eph. 5:2)

O God, help me to exercise active good will and not base my love merely on good feelings. Thank you for your continual love. Amen.

Ask God how you can learn to love someone who seems unloveable.

From Bad to Beautiful

November 27

A friend of mine once wrote a beautiful song, using the tune of a song that originally had offensive words. Even though the tune was the same, he had completely changed the meaning of the song.

This reminds me of some of the bad times I have experienced. Depending on what I do with them, they may have good or bad consequences. Like the tune of a song, events may not be bad in themselves, but how I handle them helps determine how they turn out. My responsibility is to do my best to make the most of rough situations. Christ will help transform my song of life.

For the Son of Man came to seek and to save what was lost. (Luke 19:10)

Thank you, Lord, for coming to make good out of the bad. Thank you for working in me. Amen.

What's the "tune" in your life that could use a rewrite?

Cover-Up

November 28

A layer of newly fallen snow is a beautiful sight to wake up to in the morning. All the dirt and trash are covered with a blanket of white. When it begins to melt, however, the filth is seen again.

Sometimes I try to hide the trash in my life by looking good on the outside. I may be successful for a while in the eyes of those around me, but when God takes away all that is false at the final judgment, my true nature will be visible. I must live so that nothing is covered.

"Not everyone who says to me, 'Lord, Lord,' will enter the kingdom of heaven, but only the one who does the will of my Father in heaven." (Matt. 7:21 NRSV)

Make me pure, O God, so that I won't be ashamed when every part of me is uncovered. Guide me in following your will. Amen.

Look beneath your surface with God.

———◆—◆◆—◆———

In the Noise

November 29

Some days it seems impossible to escape the noise long enough to talk to God by myself. When I'm finally alone in the quiet of my room, the phone rings, someone needs help, or the neighbors start making noise.

In loud and busy situations, it's more difficult to feel God's presence than when it's quiet and peaceful. It takes more faith to know God is with me when my conversation with him gets interrupted. But I know that whether it's noisy or quiet, God is with me.

And surely I am with you always, to the very end of the age. (Matt. 28:20)

Dear Lord, help me to remember you when I'm struggling with outside influences. Thank you that my faith doesn't need to depend on circumstances. Amen.

Practice praying in the midst of noise.

———◆—◆◆—◆———

Held by God

November 30

As the airplane flew higher into the sky, the fields, buildings, and roads became smaller. Soon white clouds surrounded the plane, and nothing else was visible.

It was the first time I had ever been in the clouds, and I felt a beautiful closeness to God. I could see nothing except the airplane that kept me up, but that was all that was necessary. This experience helped me to see that the only thing that matters in my life is the faith in God that holds me up. All my little problems seem more remote when I'm surrounded by God's love and presence.

I am the light of the world. Whoever follows me will never walk in darkness, but will have the light of life. (John 8:12)

Thank you, Jesus, for giving me the light of life. Guide me in the ways you lead. Amen.

Imagine yourself enveloped by soft clouds of God's love.

CLEO FREELANCE PHOTO

Jesus Understands   December 1

The first time our puppy's stomach growled, he jumped up and ran! Unaware that it was coming from his own stomach, he was frustrated when he couldn't escape the noise.

It sounds funny, but I wonder how many times I'm like that. Sometimes I become uneasy about my feelings, not knowing why I have them nor how to stop them. Then I remember that Jesus was once a human too and had the same feelings. He understands my feelings before I've experienced them and is always ready to help me deal with them. It's a privilege to have a protector who understands me and is willing to help me understand myself.

Praise be to the God and Father of our Lord Jesus Christ, the Father of compassion and the God of all comfort. (2 Cor. 1:3)

Thank you, Lord, for being with me when I don't understand my own feelings. Help me to accept what I can't understand without letting it hinder the rest of my life. Amen.

Tell Jesus about one confusing feeling you have.

Transforming Power   December 2

The talent of artists has always fascinated me. The way they transform simple materials, such as paper, pencils, paint, and canvas, into pieces of beauty is amazing.

Yet more amazing than any creation by a human artist is the transforming power of Christ. What looks small and worthless can be changed into something of eternal value. One life, transformed by Christ's hands, is more valuable than any piece of art a person can produce.

Do not conform any longer to the pattern of this world, but be transformed by the renewing of your mind. (Rom. 12:2)

O Christ, your power to transform lives is incredible. I invite you to make the worthless, unattractive parts of me into something beautiful. Thank you. Amen.

With what color is God painting your world today?

God Is Love   December 3

"I don't deserve God's love," a friend told me recently. She felt that she had done too many wrong things in her life and could never make it up to God. I told her that no one deserves God's love.

But I realized that subconsciously I often try to earn it too. Sometimes I try so hard to do and say the right things so I can be a good Christian. It's easy to forget that I'm loved by God even before all my efforts. God and love are the same thing! In accepting God, I accept the fact that I'm loved. All my subsequent actions are then a response to that love.

God is love. (1 John 4:16)

My God, my Love, thank you for being one in the same. Thank you, too, for giving me what I couldn't ever earn— yourself! Amen.

Be silent, close your eyes, and let yourself be enveloped in divine love.

Christ Must Be First   December 4

By holding a pencil in front of my eyes, I can block a window out of my view. By holding it closer, I can block out an entire house. It doesn't seem possible for something so small to block out a much larger object; but when each is in the right place, it can easily be done.

So it is with God. God is incomprehensibly large, but if I allow something to come between us, no matter how small, it blocks God out. Pride, money, possessions, or anything I hold dearer than Christ, diminishes my view. I must be careful to put Christ first and put everything else behind.

He is before all things, and in him all things hold together. (Col. 1:17)

Grant, O Lord, that I will not allow anything to come between us and hinder my view of you. Thank you for your help. Amen.

What is so close to your heart that it blocks a clear view of God?

Christians in Action   December 5

"Do not disturb the peace"—every citizen knows that one must obey these words to stay out of trouble with the authorities. The law is good, but many seem to have adopted it into their spiritual lives too. Often new ideas are squelched and nothing is done that will upset the status quo.

Jesus and his disciples came to turn the world upside down. They didn't teach only the things they knew would be accepted, but they spoke and lived the truth, taking the risk of being called troublemakers. I too must refuse to be content if something contradicts what I know is right in my life with Christ.

These men who have caused trouble all over the world have now come here. (Acts 17:6)

Give me guidance, Lord, to know when to speak out for you. Thank you for your example of standing up for what is right. Amen.

What do you believe in strongly enough to make you dare to be different?

Cut Off From God   December 6

As a joke, I sent a letter to my friend without signing my name. After she received it, I avoided her for the rest of the day, afraid I couldn't act normal around her and that she would figure out that I had sent it.

I did that for fun, but it's not fun when my sins cause me to avoid God. When I do something wrong, I must ask for forgiveness so our relationship can be restored. Confessing my sins to God before walls have a chance to grow between us is the only healthy way to live.

But the trouble is that your sins have cut you off from God. (Isa. 59:2 LB)

Creator God, forgive me when I allow my sins to cut me off from you. Thank you for your patience with me and your total acceptance. Amen.

Enter God's loving presence.

The Open Line   December 7

As I made the third attempt to place a long-distance phone call to a friend, I hoped a line would be open this time. I was relieved to hear the phone ring and finally the voice of my friend on the other end.

It's comforting to know that a line exists between God and me that is never too busy or overloaded for my call to get through—the channel of prayer. Even if everyone else were talking to God, my call would go through and we could communicate as well. If the line of prayer is not in use, the fault can only be my own. God is always waiting with an open line.

Those who love me, I will deliver; I will protect those who know my name. When they call to me, I will answer them." (Ps. 91:14–15 NRSV)

Thank you that the line to you is always open, Lord. Help me to remember to keep up the communication. Amen.

Imagine calling God on the phone. What will you say?

Thank God—No Flies   December 8

Last winter the thought suddenly hit me that all the flies were dead or hibernating for the winter, and none were flying around being pesky! I always knew they came out only in the summer, but I didn't really think about how nice it is not to have them around in the winter.

In the summer, when they're bothersome, I do my share of complaining about flies, but when they leave, I don't think about being thankful for their absence. This reminds me of how much I complain about things instead of praising God for the pleasures I do have.

And be thankful. (Col. 3:15)

Thank you, God that the pesky flies aren't around in the winter. Help me to look for things for which to praise you, instead of complaining. Amen.

Write a thank-you note to God.

God Is Always
Watching   December 9

When my sister and I were younger, we loved to jump on our bed. We knew we weren't allowed to do it, but when no one was in the house, we sometimes sneaked up to our room to jump anyway. We thought we were safe as long as no one caught us. Then one day the bed broke, and we were forced to admit the wrong we had done.

Sometimes I'm tempted to think that other things I do won't matter either, as long as no one sees me. But unlike my parents, God is always watching me. I must live every minute the way I want God to see me.

Live as children of light (for the fruit of the light consists in all goodness, righteousness and truth). (Eph. 5:8–9)

I appreciate your constant watching, Lord. Keep me from anything you don't approve of. Amen.

Be truthful.

Intertwining for
Support   December 10

The great redwood trees in California have always fascinated me. Some of them are 300 feet high and 2,500 years old! Since most trees have a root system that is as deep as the tree is tall, a redwood's root system could be expected to be vast, but that isn't true. It has a shallow root system. The secret of its survival is its dependence on other redwood trees. They grow in groves, so that their roots intertwine and support each other.

I often think of the greatest as being the most independent, but, as the redwood trees prove, to be great requires support from others. I shouldn't be too proud to admit my need of others. By intertwining my life with other people I can be stronger than if I try to stand alone.

So in Christ we who are many form one body, and each member belongs to all the others. (Rom. 12:5)

Thank you, Lord, for the friends you've given me with whom to intertwine my life for maximum support and strength. Amen.

Talk about your feelings with a friend.

Freedom in Christ   *December* 11

I had a classmate who became an alcoholic. He began to drink in high school as a way of expressing his freedom from authority. But the means by which he sought freedom became exactly what later enslaved him. His body was a slave to the need of alcohol.

Evil seems to promise freedom, but if I yield to it, my soul becomes stifled and imprisoned. Christ alone provides real freedom. When I turn each day over to Christ, I have freedom that cannot be found through any other means.

Restore to me again the joy of your salvation, and make me willing to obey you. (Ps. 51:12 LB)

Jesus Christ, I thank you for the freedom you've given me. Grant that I will seek freedom only in you. Amen.

Recognize your freedom.

Human Worth December 12

Each year as I hear about the large number of people killed in accidents on the highways, I am momentarily sad. It was not until one of my friends was killed, however, that I experienced the real sorrow that each death causes.

Jesus had compassion for all people because he knew the worth of each one. He came into the world to save every person and is grieved with each soul that is lost. The way to show my love for Jesus is to show compassion for everyone, just as he did.

In the same way your Father in heaven is not willing that any of these little ones should be lost. (Matt. 18:14)

Eternal God, forgive me for times I haven't cared enough about my fellow human beings. Thank you for your example of compassion. Amen.

Buy a Christmas gift for a poor child.

Wait Upon the Lord December 13

Waiting isn't easy. Everyone can testify to that from personal experiences, like waiting for a date to arrive, waiting for Christmas, waiting for a wound to heal, or waiting for the day a loved one will be seen again. These and many others are common situations people find themselves in—situations that sometimes seem unbearable.

For those who wait upon the Lord, however, renewed strength is promised. God will never faint or grow weary, and offers power to those who trust. When I learn to wait on God, I will no longer grow weary. God helps me endure trials and hardships.

Those who hope in the Lord will renew their strength. They will soar on wings like eagles; they will run and not grow weary; they will walk and not be faint. (Isa. 40:31)

Teach me, Lord, to wait upon you for all my needs. Give me patience as I wait. Amen.

Turn your waiting into prayer.

Individuality   December 14

An interesting place our family sometimes stops to visit has bushes all over the yard. Each bush has been trimmed into the shape of a different animal. The bushes, which had been alike and ordinary before, were brought to life when someone took the time to make each one unique.

God has taken the time to make each person unique too. The variety the great Artist provides makes life interesting. By trying to be just like someone else, I'm ruining God's tremendous act of creativity.

Does not the potter have the right to make out of the same lump of clay some pottery for noble purposes and some for common use? (Rom. 9:21)

O God, thank you for caring enough to make me a unique individual. Thank you that I don't have to try to be like anyone else. Amen.

Celebrate your uniqueness!

It Is the Lord!   December 15

Jesus appeared to his disciples several times after he rose from the dead. On one such occasion, he stood on the shore, calling to those who were fishing on the lake. John was the first to recognize him. He knew that only Jesus could cause their nets to be full of fish.

When Jesus appears today, too often I fail to recognize him. When I look, I can see Christ in birds, people, trees, attitudes, and circumstances. Then I have the opportunity to say, "It is the Lord!"

Then the disciple whom Jesus loved said to Peter, "It is the Lord!" (John 21:7)

Thank you, Lord, for making yourself real to me in many situations. Grant that I will recognize you more often in the details of each day. Amen.

Look for the Lord.

Heart to Heart   December 16

December is a busy month as people prepare for the Christmas season. At this time of the year, as at any busy time, I need to make a special effort to spend some time each day with my Lord. It's not always easy to take time, but if I'm sincere, it's always worthwhile.

I am inspired by the words of Henry Drummond: "Five minutes spent in the companionship of Christ every morning, aye, two minutes, if it is face to face and heart to heart, will change the whole day."

I screamed, "I'm slipping, Lord!" and he was kind and saved me. (Ps. 94:18 LB)

Forgive me, O Christ, for the times when I should have stopped to talk to you but didn't. Thank you for helping me when I ask for your guidance and for being patient when I forget. Amen.

Spend two minutes face to face and heart to heart with Christ.

God's Presence   December 17

I once heard a story about a visiting preacher who wondered why the church in which he was preaching smelled so good. Upon asking for the secret, he learned that most of the people of that congregation worked in a perfume factory. The aroma stayed with them and gave fragrance to the entire church building.

If I spend time in God's presence, it will affect those around me, just as the fragrance of the perfume was evident on the factory workers. The distinctive qualities of love and goodness will radiate from me. Only by living in God's presence can I show forth the Holy Spirit.

For in him we live and move and have our being. (Acts 17:28)

I pray, Lord, that your presence in me will be evident to all those around me. May I keep it that way by remaining in your presence. Amen.

Radiate God's fragrance.

Snowflakes   December 18

A snowflake is a beautiful phenomenon. Some people may not like countless snowflakes piled up and in need of being shoveled off the sidewalks, and they may not like the coldness that accompanies them, but each separate flake is a marvelously intricate work of art. They all look alike until they're observed more closely. Then it becomes clear that each one is different. If God cares enough to send something as beautiful as a snowflake to me, even though I often neglect to enjoy its beauty, how much God must care for me!

O Lord, what a variety you have made! And in wisdom you have made them all! The earth is full of your riches. (Ps. 104:24 LB)

Lord, your artwork is fantastic! Thank you for the beauty in small everyday things. Amen.

Make a paper snowflake.

The Greatest King   December 19

Jesus came quietly into the world of which he was to become King. Few people were expecting the arrival of the One whose name would be exalted above all names, but that didn't seem to bother anyone. Joseph and Mary calmly accepted a stable for his birth, the shepherds rejoiced, and the Magi chose not to spread the news to Herod.

Many didn't recognize Jesus as the greatest person ever born—in fact, many rejected him—but that didn't make his life worth any less. When I'm tempted to feel rejected and worthless, I can remember how the greatest One who ever lived was also rejected.

The stone the builders rejected has become the capstone; the Lord has done this, and it is marvelous in our eyes. (Mark 12:10–11)

Jesus, my Lord, help me to see that to be the greatest doesn't mean that I'll always be accepted. Teach me to do your will. Amen.

Make another feel accepted.

Obedience with Offering

December 20

The Christmas season finds people doing many nice things—sending cards of appreciation to friends, giving the newspaper carrier an extra tip, singing carols to the elderly and the poor, giving gifts, and baking for lots of company. All of these are enjoyable as well as good; but I need to ask myself in the midst of it all if what I'm doing is really honoring Jesus.

Examples in the Bible teach that God doesn't always accept offerings. God is not interested in them unless obedience is also given. I must ask myself if in all the Christmas activities I'm trying to impress people or obey God.

Obedience is far better than sacrifice. (1 Sam. 15:22 LB)

Dear Jesus, let me not think good acts alone will please you. Guide me in keeping your will in all that I do. Amen.

Listen for how God would like you to celebrate the Christmas spirit.

What Did You Give?

December 21

"What did you get for Christmas?"

"Did you get everything you wanted?"

These kinds of questions are not uncommon after Christmas gifts are opened. I had asked them many times myself until last year when a new thought struck me. A friend and I were wondering why we ask people these questions if we truly believe the verse that says it is more blessed to give than to receive. We decided instead to ask people what they *gave* for Christmas. At first many were caught off guard because it wasn't the normal question, and they began to tell what they'd received. But when they finally caught on, their smiles showed that they, too, understood that what is given is the most important.

It is more blessed to give than to receive. (Acts 20:35)

Thank you, Lord, for the resources I have from which I can give to others. Keep me mindful of the importance of giving. Amen.

Give a homemade Christmas gift.

Be a Good Receiver   December 22

Even though it is more blessed to give than to receive, it is also a necessary skill to be able to receive graciously. I have always gotten joy out of giving, but until recently I didn't realize the importance of being willing to receive.

A friend and I were eating at a restaurant one evening. To show my appreciation of her friendship, I wanted to pay for her meal, but she refused my offer. She insisted that she could afford it better than I could. She didn't realize the joy I would have had in doing it or the hurt I felt when I was turned down.

From that incident I've learned how crucial it is to be a good receiver. This Christmas especially I want to make my appreciation more evident.

If a man's gift is . . . contributing to the needs of others, let him give generously. (Rom. 12:6–7)

Grant, O God, that I will be a gracious receiver. Teach me the joy of receiving as well as giving. Amen.

Appreciate those who give to you.

More Than a Celebration

As Christmas draws near and celebrations, pretty decorations, and parties are at their height, it's easy to become caught up in the activities and forget the true meaning of Christmas. The traditional manger scene of the baby Jesus is beautiful, and everyone loves the story of his birth and enjoys praising God for sending his Son.

But the enthusiasm is lost after Christmas when we study Jesus' growth and ministry. Adoring the baby Jesus is easier than following Jesus as Lord. Christmas is much more than a joyful celebration; it is a plea for a mature commitment to Christ to be Jesus' representative on earth.

And a voice from heaven said, "This is my Son, whom I love; with him I am well pleased." (Matt. 3:17)

Son of God, guide me in my love for you, that you will be glorified as Lord, not just adored as a baby. Amen.

Read Luke 1:26–38.

The Best Thing That Happened

December 24

When I see a beautiful view, hear a good joke, or experience something new and exciting, my first reaction is to share it with someone. I can't keep all the joy to myself.

Neither could the angels keep their joy suppressed when Jesus was born. Many came from heaven to tell the shepherds of his glory. Jesus' birth and entrance into my life is the greatest thing that has happened to me. If I long to share many smaller things with my friends, how much more should

I be sharing with them the good news of Jesus—especially if they don't know it yet.

Christmas is a good time to begin telling those I come in contact with about the best thing that has happened in my life.

And suddenly there was with the angel a multitude of the heavenly host, praising God and saying, "Glory to God in the highest heaven, and on earth peace among those whom he favors." (Luke 2:13–14 NRSV)

Thank you, God, for sending your Son to the world. Guide me in sharing the good news of Jesus' birth and life with those around me. Amen.

Read Luke 2:1–20.

Love Gifts   December 25

Every year my sister and I try to surprise Mother with a birthday cake. And every year something goes wrong, and the cake is a flop. But Mother always acts as if it's the best cake she's ever tasted. She appreciates the love that went into making it and hardly notices that we messed it up.

On Christmas, when I like to give gifts, I must remember the lesson she taught me. A gift, no matter how small or inexpensive, is worth much if I give it out of love. Just as God gave Jesus in love, I want to give in love.

Above all, love each other deeply, because love covers over a multitude of sins. (1 Peter 4:8)

Thank you, Father, for Jesus—the most loving gift I have ever received. May I give gifts with the same loving attitude. Amen.

Read Matthew 2:1–12.

Christmas Isn't Over   December 26

Christmas Day is past for another year, but is Christmas over?

I like what Dale Evans Rogers says about it: "Christmas, my child, is love in action. . . . When you love someone, you give to them, as God gives to us. The greatest gift God ever gave was the Person of Jesus, sent to us in human form so that we might know what God is really like! Every time we love, every time we give, it's Christmas."

So December 25 is really just a take-off point for countless more Christmas experiences throughout the coming year!

For unto us a Child is born; . . . These will be his royal titles: "Wonderful," "Counselor," "The Mighty God," "The Everlasting Father," "The Prince of Peace." (Isa. 9:6 LB)

Thank you, Jesus, not only for one but for 365 days of Christmas a year. Amen.

Review last year's New Year's resolutions.

———————•◦———◦•———

Unearned Love   December 27

When someone does me a favor, I often feel as if I don't deserve it, and I try to think of how to repay the kindness. True love, however, is never earned; it must be given. God's love and forgiveness are difficult for my human mind to conceive of. They are gifts to each one who has enough faith to believe. Doing things for God must be a result of our relationship, not a way to earn his friendship.

For it is by grace you have been saved, through faith—and this not from yourselves, it is the gift of God. (Eph. 2:8)

Thank you, God, for your gifts of love and forgiveness. Grant that I will not try to earn these gifts but that I will act in a loving way because of them. Amen.

Rest in God's gift of love.

The Cross   December 28

A few years ago I received a cross necklace from a friend. It was to remind me of the power I could have from Jesus when I was willing to ask him to guide my life. The cross became a reminder of Jesus' life of continual giving.

Christmas and Easter are closely tied together. Jesus came to give his life for the sins of the world. Therefore, to be a follower means that I, too, must be willing to give of myself for Christ's purposes.

I appeal to you therefore, brothers and sisters, by the mercies of God, to present your bodies as a living sacrifice, holy and acceptable to God, which is your spiritual worship. (Rom. 12:1 NRSV)

Dear Jesus, keep me ever mindful of the need to give myself to your work. Thank you for the privilege of receiving your mercy. Amen.

Find a reminder of Jesus' power in your life.

Love at Home   December 29

We sometimes sing the hymn "Love at Home." The first line says, "There is beauty all around when there's love at home."

I often take the love I have at home for granted. Love in the broader sense, in the Christian family, is sometimes taken for granted too. I forget that without love, there could be no real beauty. Jesus was born to bring God's love to the world. Through that divine love, I can have real joy and beauty.

Therefore love is the fulfillment of the law. (Rom. 13:10)

Thank you, almighty God, for your love, which surrounds me with beauty. May I be a useful channel through which to keep love alive. Amen.

Be aware of all the ways you are loved at home.

———◦●——●●——●◦———

Revolution in Resolutions   December 30

As this year comes to a close, many people are making resolutions for the year to come. Whether this past year was a good one or one marked with many failures, everyone hopes the new year will be better. High hopes are also put on a better life in the Lord. But why are good intentions so often not carried out?

Part of the reason may be that the resolutions don't become revolutions. I resolve that I want God to control my life, but I forget to let God make a revolution of my life. In the coming year I don't want to merely make resolutions but also to let God turn them into revolutions.

And I will give you a new heart—I will give you new and right desires—and put a new spirit within you. (Ezek. 36:26 LB)

Mold my life, O God, in the coming year. Turn the good intentions of my resolutions into revolutions in my life. Amen.

Write in your journal one way your life could be revolutionized in the coming year.

Inventory December 31

Another year is almost over. It's time to look back over the past year and see what needs to be changed in my life.

More important, it's time to look ahead and be ready for all the things God has in store for me in the coming year. Each year has more in it than I'm ready to handle alone, but with Jesus as a constant friend to help me with each step, it will be the best year yet.

He has delivered us from such a deadly peril, and he will deliver us. On him we have set our hope that he will continue to deliver us. (2 Cor. 1:10)

Lord, I commit the coming year to your work in my life, and I commit my life to you to use in whatever way you desire. Amen.

Thank God for the gifts of the past year.